COMPUTERS

STEPHEN BENNINGTON

CONSULTANT: PAUL FISHER

LORENZ BOOKS

First published by Lorenz Books in 2001

© 2001 Anness Publishing Limited

Published in the USA by Lorenz Books
Anness Publishing Inc.
27 West 20th Street
New York
NY 10011

Lorenz Books is an imprint of Anness Publishing Inc.

www.lorenzbooks.com

Publisher: Joanna Lorenz
Managing Editor, Children's Books: Gilly Cameron Cooper
Senior Editor: Lisa Miles
Editor: Leon Gray
Assistant Editor: Jenni Rainford
Consultant: Paul Fisher
Creative Consultant: Sarah Richardson
Jacket Design: Joyce Mason
Designer: Micheal Leaman
Photographer: John Freeman
Picture Researchers: Gwen Campbell and Penni Bickle
Illustrator: Guy Smith
Editorial Reader: Kate Humby
Production Controller: Claire Rae

10 9 8 7 6 5 4 3 2 1

The publishers would like to thank the following children
for modeling in this book: Emily Askew, Sara Barnes, Maria
Bloodworth, David Callega, Aaron Dumetz, Laurence de Freitas,
Alistair Fulton, Anton Goldbourne, Sasha Howarth, Jon Leming,
Jessica Moxley, Ifunanya Obi, Emily Preddie, Elen Rhys,
Nicola Twiner, Joe Westbrook.

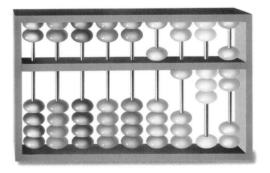

PICTURE CREDITS
b=bottom, t=top, c=center, l=left, r=right
Adobe: 3cl, 3bl, 3bcr, 19 (x3) • Courtesy of Apple Computers, Inc.: 6br, 9cr, 9bcr, 13t, 13b, 18c, 19tr, 19bl, 19tr (x2), 50, 51
• Casio: 61tl • Corbis – AFP: 53b; Kevin Fleming: 22b, 57b • Diablo II: 39bl • Getty One Stone – Chad Slattery: 57t; Lonny
Kalfus: cover l; Nicholas Veasey: back cover cr, Peter Dazeley: 4c & 5c (in monitor), 13bc (in monitor); Peter Poulides: cover c,
3tcr, 14bc • Hulton Getty: 9bl • Iomega® Zip: 4bc, 15br • Louvre Museum – 54b (x3), 55t (x4), 55c (x2); ©Photo
RMN/R. G. Ojeda: 54tr • Mary Evans Picture Library: 8bl • Mattel Interactive: 41t • Microsoft Corporation – Microsoft®
Word: 3tcl, 18bl (x4); Microsoft® Windows®: 19br, 19tl (x2); Microsoft Clip Art: 24b (x4) • Netscape Communications:
2cr, 3bcl, 19 (x1) • Olympus Cameras: 28c • Powerstock Photo Library/Zefa: 1, 38tl • Robert Partridge: The Ancient Egypt
Picture Library: 54c • Science and Society Picture Library – Bletchley Park Trust: 9tl; J.-L. Charmet: 8tl; Science Museum:
8cl, 9tr, 9tcl, 22t • Science Photo Library – 57c; Alex Bartel: 4c, 5c; Caida: 48c; CS Langlois/Publiphoto Diffusion: 46bl;
D. Parker: 53c; Damien Lovegrove: cover br, 42b; David Ducros: 48tl; De Renpentigny/Publiphoto: 56br; Gable Jerrican: 49;
Hank Morgan: 42c, 46tr; J. L. Charmet: 8tl; James King-Holmes: 45cl, 56bl; James King-Holmes/W Industries: back cover cl,
44tl; Jerry Mason: 40bl, 56tl, 60tr; Dr. Jurgen Scriba: 29c; Peter Menzel: cover br, 39br, 44cr, 45cr; Ph. Plailly/Eurelios: 45tl;
Sam Ogden: 3br, 38bl, 44bl, 52t, 60cr, 60bl; Dr. Seth Shostak: back cover br; Tek Image: 6br (in monitor), 42tl, 61cl;
Tom Van Sant Geosphere Project/Planetary Visions: 48bl; Tony Craddock: 8br, 37b; Volker Steger: 10, 45br • Sim City
2000: 39cr • Sony: 2t, 5tr, 36tr, 38cr, 40tl, 61b, 62 • Trip – J. Okwesa: 2b, 9bbcr; A. Gigg: 4cl, 9tcr; H. Rosens: 31bl;
J. Lamb: 35cr • VA Linux Systems: 18tl • Victoria and Albert Picture Library: 55b • Yahoo!, Inc.: 52; 53t.

Computer art courtesy of Stephen Bennington

INVESTIGATIONS

COMPUTERS

CONTENTS

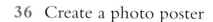

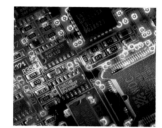

COMPUTER BASICS

THOUSANDS of everyday tasks are now much easier to do thanks to the development of computers. Many activities, such as writing, drawing, playing music, sending messages, playing games, looking up information and even shopping are regularly done using these powerful machines. Living in today's computer age means that almost everyone has access to the technology—in offices, schools, stores and at home. Indeed, computers are such an integral part of modern society that it is hard to imagine how humans once coped without them.

monitor

Some people believe that computers can think like people. In fact, they can only use information that is put into them. The most important job computers do is to process such information much more quickly and accurately than a person could. Performing complex calculations, checking for spelling mistakes in a story or copying pictures from one place to another, for example, are done much faster using a computer. Essentially, computers are just tools like washing machines and cars. They are used in many different ways to do an enormous range of interesting and useful tasks.

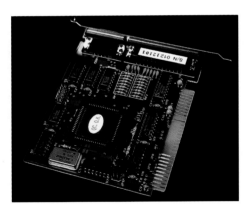

Disks and data
Data (information) can be stored on disks outside the main part of the computer. The disk can be in the form of a CD (compact disc), DVD (digital versatile disc), Zip disk or floppy disk. These are placed in different slots, called drives, in the computer to allow new data to be put in and recorded data to be taken out.

Processing power
The computer's brain, where data is handled and rearranged, is called the processor. This is a complicated electronic circuit board, which contains smaller electronic circuits called silicon chips. These chips are the powerhouses of all computers. They contain other electronic circuits that are so small that they can only be seen under a microscope.

Storage system

The hard drive is the computer's storage unit where all the data it needs is kept. It consists of a set of spinning disks and a moving arm that reads what is stored there. We cannot see the hard drive because it needs to be enclosed in a box to keep it free from dust.

hard drive

speaker

Play the game

A joystick, gamepad or steering wheel are sometimes needed to play computer games. They are easier to use than a mouse for this purpose, and they make the game feel more real. For instance, using a steering wheel to play a driving game makes it feel as if you are really driving.

Sound it out

Most computers have a built-in speaker, but external speakers add to the quality of the sound. External speakers come in a range of shapes and sizes and have to be able to generate all kinds of sounds, from CD-quality stereo to movie soundtracks.

Mouse clicks

The mouse is used to control the pointer, or cursor, on the screen. The pointer moves according to the direction the mouse moves. You press part of the mouse to do a range of tasks, such as moving objects. Pressing the mouse is called clicking.

keyboard *mouse* *mouse pad*

Hard copy

A printer translates what you see on screen, such as pages of text or pictures, onto paper. Modern inkjet color printers can produce photographic-quality prints, but black-and-white laser printers are most commonly used in offices.

Scan it

A scanner turns ordinary pictures on paper, such as photos from a book, into a form that the computer can read. The scanner analyzes the image and sends the data to the computer in a form that it can read.

ALL TALK

EVERY subject uses a set of words and phrases, called jargon, to describe things that have not existed before. This is certainly true when you start exploring the world of computers. Computer jargon is usually made up of either new scientific terms, such as "computer," or existing words that have been given a new meaning, such as "mouse." They can also be words made from the first letters of phrases, such as "PC," which stands for Personal Computer. These are called acronyms. One of the main reasons people have difficulty with learning a new subject, and even give the subject up, is because they come across a lot of new and confusing words that they do not fully understand. If you are not sure what a word means then you will probably find it in the Glossary at the end of this book. If not, then you are bound to find it in an up-to-date dictionary. Knowing what computer jargon means when you see and hear it is very important. Remember that everyone is in the same position when they learn about a new subject. You will gradually pick up what each new word means as you read and learn more about it. The boxes on the opposite page will start you off with some essential computer jargon.

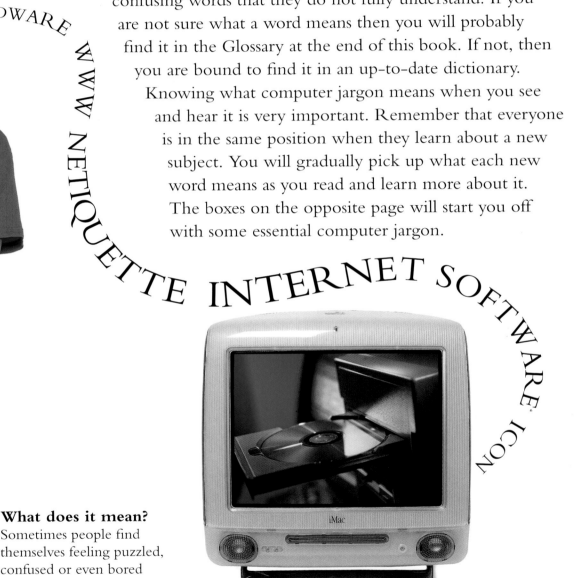

What does it mean?
Sometimes people find themselves feeling puzzled, confused or even bored when they try to learn about computers. These feelings often come from not fully understanding the many new and sometimes strange words that are associated with the subject.

Speaking the language
Lots of unusual words and phrases are used to describe computers. For example, the piece of equipment above is called a monitor, and it displays computer data on a screen much like a television. The monitor above shows a CD-ROM. Do you know what CD-ROM stands for?

SOME FIRST JARGON WORDS

- **Hardware** – Equipment, such as the processor, monitor, keyboard, scanner, and mouse, that makes up your computer system.

- **Home page** – An introductory page on a web site, that contains links to other pages.

- **Icon** – A small picture that you can click on with the mouse to make the computer do something.

- **Internet** – A worldwide computer network, through which computers can communicate with each other.

- **Netiquette** – A code of good conduct and manners, developed by Internet users, that suggests acceptable and unacceptable ways of behaving on the Internet.

- **Software** – A set of coded instructions, called an application, that tells your computer what to do.

- **Web site** – A computer document written in HTML (see right), that is linked to other computer documents.

INTERNET

A worldwide computer network, through which computers communicate with each other.

A helping hand

There are many ways to find out about computers and the jargon that comes with using them. Your family and friends may be able to help, or you could join a computer club and meet lots of other people who are trying to find out about computers. You could even use the Internet to try and answer your questions.

EASY ACRONYMS

Here are some common acronyms that you will come across regularly.

- **CD-ROM** (**C**ompact **D**isc **R**ead-**O**nly **M**emory) – A disk similar to an audio CD, that contains information that can only be read by the computer.

- **CPU** (**C**entral **P**rocessing **U**nit) – The brain of the computer, that contains the processing chips and circuit boards.

- **HTML** (**H**yper**T**ext **M**ark-up **L**anguage) – A computer code that is added to word-processed documents to turn them into web pages.

- **ISP** (**I**nternet **S**ervice **P**rovider) – The companies through which Internet connection is made.

- **Modem** (**MO**dulator/ **DEM**odulator) – A device that allows computer information to be sent through a telephone line.

- **RAM** (**R**andom **A**ccess **M**emory) – Computer memory that holds information temporarily until the computer is switched off.

- **URL** (**U**niform **R**esource **L**ocator) – The address of a site on the Internet that is specific to one web page.

- **WWW** (**W**orld **W**ide **W**eb) – A huge collection of information that is available on the Internet. The information comprises of web sites, that are made up of many web pages.

HISTORY OF COMPUTERS

Blaise Pascal's calculator
In 1642, French mathematician Blaise Pascal invented the first automatic calculator. The device added and subtracted by means of a set of wheels linked by gears. The first wheel represented the numbers 0 to 9, the second wheel represented 10s, the third stood for 100s, and so on. When the first wheel was turned ten notches, a gear moved the second wheel forward a notch and so on.

THE idea of using machines to do automated tasks and calculations is not a new one. The first calculating machine was developed in the 1600s and used moving parts such as wheels, cogs and gears to do mathematical tasks. The first big step towards developing an automatic computing machine came about in 1801. Joseph-Marie Jacquard, a French weaver, invented a weaving machine that was controlled by a series of punched cards. Where there were holes, the needles rose and met the thread, but where there were no holes, the needles were blocked. This was the first time that stored information had been used to work a machine.

Early in the 1900s, electronic devices began to replace mechanical (hand-operated) machines. These computers filled an entire room, yet they could only perform simple calculations. In later years, two main inventions—the transistor in the 1950s and the silicon chip in the 1970s—allowed the modern computer to be developed. Both of these devices control tiny electrical currents that give computers instructions. Today, computers can be made to fit in the palm of your hand.

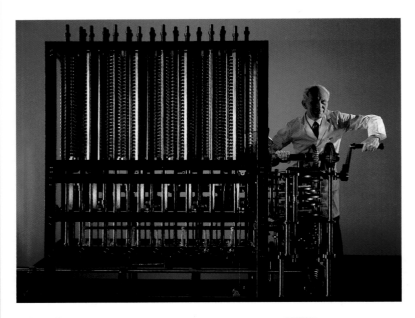

Mechanical mathematics
In 1835, British mathematician Charles Babbage invented a mechanical calculating machine called the Analytical Engine. When performing calculations, the machine stored completed sets of punched cards that were reusable. The Analytical Engine had all the elements of a modern computer—storage, memory, a system for moving between the two and an input device. The people who used his machines were called "computers."

The first programmer
Ada, Countess of Lovelace, was the daughter of English poet Lord Byron and probably the world's first computer programmer. Between 1833 and 1843, she became interested in the work of fellow mathematician Charles Babbage. She created a punchcard program that was used to record the data for Babbage's Analytical Engine.

Controlling the current
Today, computers work by electrical currents that flow through circuits. The current is controlled by devices called transistors. These are found on a wafer-thin piece of silicon called a chip. Some chips are no larger than a fingernail and contain millions of transistors. These are known as integrated circuits (ICs).

Code cracker

During World War II, British mathematician Alan Mathison Turing developed the first fully electronic calculating device. It was called Colossus because of its huge size. This machine was equipped with over 1,500 vacuum tubes that were used to control thousands of electrical currents. Colossus was designed to decipher a German communications code called Enigma. The machine was successful and helped Britain and its Allies win World War II (1939–1945). Colossus can still be seen at the Bletchley Park Museum in the United Kingdom, the site where the code-cracking operation took place.

Two-room calculator

In 1943, ENIAC (Electronic Numerical Integrator and Computer) was constructed by Presper Eckert, John Atansoff, and John Mauchly at the University of Pennsylvania. This early computer was enormous, filling two rooms and using as much electricity as ten family houses. It contained about 18,000 vacuum tubes, that acted as electronic switches and could perform hundreds of calculations every second. ENIAC was slow to program, however, because thousands of wires and connections had to be changed by hand.

COMPUTER DEVELOPMENTS

Television link
British inventor Sir Clive Sinclair developed many personal computers, including the ZX80 in 1980. This used a normal television as a monitor.

All in one
The Commodore 8032-SK was launched in 1980 and was the first computer to have a built-in monitor to display information.

BBC Model B
The BBC Model B was launched in 1981 by British computer firm Acorn to accompany the British Broadcasting Company (BBC) computer literacy program.

Laptop
International Business Machines Corporation (IBM) was instrumental in the development of a portable computer, called a laptop, in the early 1990s.

iMac
The iMac, developed by Apple Computers, revolutionized the design of desktop computers when it appeared on the market in the late 1990s.

iBook
Apple introduced the iBook in 1999. As powerful as a desktop iMac, this portable model also comes in a variety of bright, attractive colors.

Palm Pilot
A hand-held, pocket-size computer appeared in the late 90s. Not only does it feature an electronic pen for writing directly on the screen, it can also connect to the Internet.

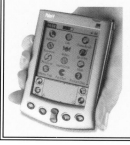

BREAKING THE CODE

COMPUTERS are digital machines, which means they work by using a sequence of alternating numbers. The word "digit" actually means a counting finger, but it is used in computing to mean every single number between 0 and 9.

The number code that computers use is called binary code, which means it is made up of just two digits—0 and 1 (binary means two). Combinations of 0 and 1 can be used to represent any kind of information, for example, the letters of the alphabet. The theory behind this binary code is essentially the same as the one that Joseph-Marie Jacquard used for the punched cards that worked his weaving looms. Jacquard's punched cards were used to represent two kinds of information—a hole (1 in binary code) or no hole (0 in binary code).

Coded messages

This device, called the Enigma machine, was used by German forces during World War II (1939–1945). Uncoded messages were typed into the keyboard, and the machine then converted the message into a complex coded form. So complex was Enigma that a single letter could be represented by several different coded characters.

BINARY CODE

A	01000001	N	01001110	0	00110000
B	01000010	O	01001111	1	00110001
C	01000011	P	01010000	2	00110010
D	01000100	Q	01010001	3	00110011
E	01000101	R	01010010	4	00110100
F	01000110	S	01010011	5	00110101
G	01000111	T	01010100	6	00110110
H	01001000	U	01010101	7	00110111
I	01001001	V	01010110	8	00111000
J	01001010	W	01010111	9	00111001
K	01001011	X	01011000	10	00111010
L	01001100	Y	01011001		
M	01001101	Z	01011010		

Zeros and ones

Binary code is the language that all computers use in their calculations. Computers understand the code in terms of an electrical current (flow of electricity). An electrical current being on or off is represented by 0 and 1. In computing, zeros are used to mean off and ones are used to mean on. In this way, binary code can be used to represent all kinds of different information on a computer. For example, it can be used to represent decimal numbers or the letters of the alphabet, as shown in the chart on the left. Computers recognize each number or letter as a group of eight binary digits. Combinations of binary digits represent different numbers or letters.

A STRING OF BITS

You will need: *16 small pieces of colored paper, black marker, stencil, two 3-ft lengths of string, 16 clothes pegs.*

1 Look at the binary code version of the alphabet on the opposite page. See how many 0s and 1s you need to represent the initials of your name. Use a black marker and a stencil to draw them on the paper.

2 Arrange the 0s and 1s in two rows, one for each initial of your name. Each piece of paper represents a bit. This is the smallest amount of digital information in a computer.

3 When you have finished, double-check with the chart opposite to make sure you have got the 0s and 1s in the right place. The group of eight bits that represents each letter of the alphabet is called a byte.

4 Take the two pieces of string and the clothes pegs. Peg each bit to the string in the correct order, putting your first initial letter on one piece of string and your second initial on the other piece. The example in the picture shows the binary code version of the letters P and C.

GETTING STUFF IN AND OUT

COMPUTERS can only work with the information that you put into them. The main way that you put information into a computer is by using a keyboard and a mouse. The mouse controls the cursor (a movable visible point) on the monitor and allows you to select different options. The keys on a keyboard have one or more characters printed on them, such as a letter or a number. When you press a key, the main character on the key will appear on the screen. Other keys on the keyboard are used to give the computer specific instructions. There are two main types of home computer—a PC (personal computer) and a Mac (Apple Macintosh—named after the company that developed it). Their keyboards are slightly different, but they do the same jobs.

You can see the work you have created as words, numbers or pictures on the computer's monitor. You can print it on paper, save it on the hard disk or save it to a removable disk at any time.

It is a good idea to save your work every few minutes so that it is firmly recorded. If anything should go wrong with the computer, the data that you have not saved will be lost and you will have to redo all the work you have done.

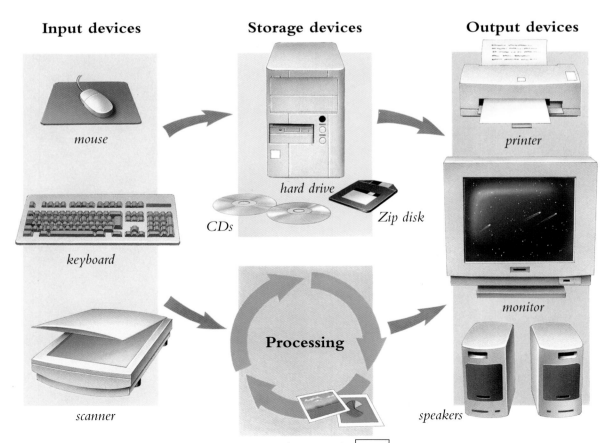

Input devices

mouse

keyboard

scanner

Storage devices

hard drive

CDs

Zip disk

Processing

Output devices

printer

monitor

speakers

Using computers
When people use a computer, they are doing four different things:

1. Inputting data (information) using an input device.

2. Storing the data so that it can be reused (often called data storage).

3. Working with the data they put in (often called processing).

4. Retrieving and looking at the data using an output device.

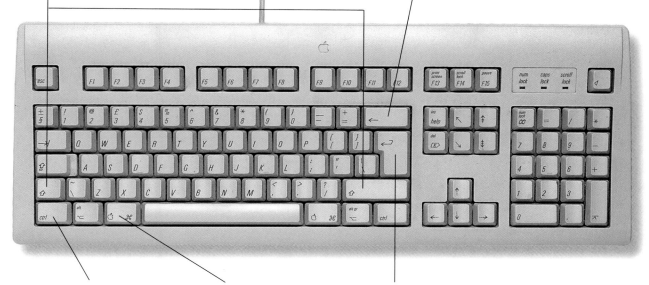

*The **Shift** key is used in combination with a letter key to type a capital letter. It is also used in some keyboard shortcuts to tell a computer to do a specific task.*

*The **Back Space** key is used to remove selected words or images in an application.*

The keyboard

All keyboards do the same jobs, although some are designed differently from others. The one shown here is a Mac keyboard. You can also buy ergonomic keyboards, that are designed to suit the human body. The keys fit the natural positions and movements of the user's hands, avoiding muscle strain.

*The **Control** key is used with different letter keys to tell the computer to do different tasks.*

*The **Apple** key is a special key that can be found on the keyboards of Macs. It is used together with letter keys to do specific tasks. On a PC, the **Windows** key does the same job.*

*Pressing the **Enter** key on a keyboard is like saying OK to the computer. This key is also used in typing for taking words over to the next line.*

Monitors

As you input information to the computer, the results of your actions appear on the screen of a monitor. The picture on the screen is made up of small dots of light called pixels. Some monitors can display more pixels than others, that produces a better-quality picture on screen. These monitors are said to have a high resolution.

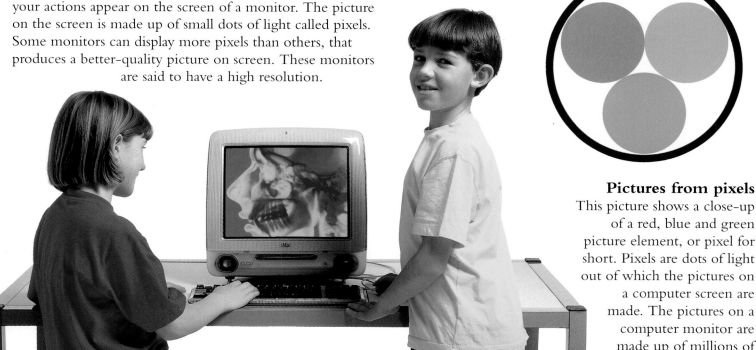

Pictures from pixels

This picture shows a close-up of a red, blue and green picture element, or pixel for short. Pixels are dots of light out of which the pictures on a computer screen are made. The pictures on a computer monitor are made up of millions of red, blue and green pixels.

STORING AND FINDING

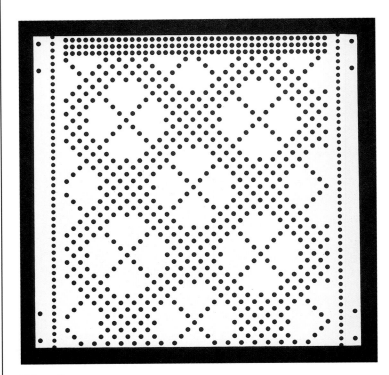

The first computer program
The punched cards that Joseph-Marie Jacquard used in 1801 to operate his weaving machine worked in exactly the same way as the electrical impulses in binary code. The needles could pass through a hole in the card to meet the thread and make a stitch (equivalent to the binary digit 1, or on), but they were blocked if there was no hole (equivalent to the binary digit 0, or off). In this way, different patterns of holes on the punched cards represented different patterns of woven cloth.

Ticker tape
Ticker tape was first used in the 1930s by German scientist Konrad Zuse. Holes were punched in the tape in the same way as Jacquard's cards, but the tape was fed into the computer as a continuous strip. A hole was read as the binary digit 1. No hole was read as the binary digit 0. The smaller holes held the tape in the machine.

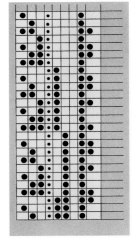

THE part of the computer that does all the calculations is called the microprocessor. It consists of millions of electronic switches, called transistors, and other electronic devices that are all built into a wafer-thin slice of a chemical element called silicon. Electricity passes through tiny lines of metal on the silicon chip. The transistors switch the electricity on and off. These on-and-off pulses of electricity represent the 0s and 1s of binary code, which the computer interprets to do different tasks.

Microprocessors control a number of other devices besides computers, including telephones, car engines and thermostats (heat-control devices) on washing machines.

Silicon chips control other devices in a computer such as memory chips. These store information that is needed by the microprocessor to run software such as a word-processing application. Other data is stored on various kinds of disks, including hard disks, floppy disks, Zip disks and CDs.

Memory chips
There are two basic kinds of memory chips in a modern computer. RAM (random-access memory) chips remember information only when the computer is switched on. When you turn your computer off, everything on the RAM chip is erased. RAM chips provide the space your computer needs to run software. ROM (read-only memory) chips remember information permanently. They store essential data, such as the program that enables your computer to start up.

land   pit

FACT BOX

• The amount of digital information that the memory chips or storage disks can hold is measured in bits and bytes (words derived from **bi**nary dig**it**s).

• A bit can be either a 0 or a 1. Computers read information as a sequence of eight bits of code, which is equivalent to a byte (an average-length word). A kilobyte (KB or K) is one thousand bytes. A megabyte (MB) is one million bytes. A gigabyte (GB) is one billion bytes.

• A modern hard disk can store well over 10 gigabytes, which is the equivalent of over 20 million paperback books. Hard drives are getting bigger all the time.

• Magnetic tape drives are another way of saving large files from your computer. The drive can be installed inside or outside a computer, and it has a large capacity— enough to hold all the data on an entire hard drive.

CD (Compact Disc)

Data is recorded on to a compact disc by a laser beam cutting into a thin metal layer under the plastic coating of the disk. The disk becomes covered with microscopic indentations (pits) and flat areas (lands). These are read by another laser in the computer. The pits are read as binary 1 and the lands as binary 0. Most CD-ROMs can store around 750MB of information.

Storing data

Magnetic disks, such as the computer's hard disk, floppy disks and Zip disks, store data arranged in a circular track. This is divided into sections, like pieces of pie, to make compartments. A device in the computer, called the read/write head, moves from one section to another to read or change the data. Hard disks have the largest storage capacity, and they are the most popular way of storing information.

Floppy disk

These disks are made of thin magnetic plastic encased in a stiff plastic shell. The plastic inside the disk stores a pattern of 1s and 0s in the form of magnetic particles. Floppy disks can store up to 1.4MB of data, which is the same as three paperback books. Floppy disks are becoming less popular as a way of saving and sending information due to their small capacity.

Zip disk

Like floppy disks, Zip disks use magnetism to store data, but are able to hold about 80 times as much information. Although about the same size as a floppy disk, they hold between 100 and 250 MB of data (about the same as 80 floppy disks). Zip disks are a very useful way of storing large computer files, and many people use these disks to back up all the files on their computer's hard disk.

HARD DISK STORAGE

THE hard disk of a computer consists of a number of flat, circular plates. Each one of these plates is coated with microscopic magnetic particles. The hard disk also contains a controlling mechanism, called the read/write head, which is positioned slightly above the magnetic disks.

When storing information, a series of electrical pulses representing the data are sent through the read/write head onto the magnetic disks, which are spinning at very high speeds. The electricity magnetizes the magnetic particles on the disks, which then align to produce a record of the signal.

When reading information, the hard disk works in the opposite way. The magnetic particles create a small current, which is recognized by the read/write head, converted into an electrical current and then into binary code.

When you load new information onto the computer, it is stored in a section of one of the plates, depending on where there is free space. The computer then keeps a record of what is stored in each section. This project shows you how the magnetic disks in your computer's hard drive work.

STORING DATA ON A DISK

You will need: *piece of white card stock, compass, pencil, scissors, ruler, red marker, plastic cup, reusable adhesive, paper clips, magnet, tack.*

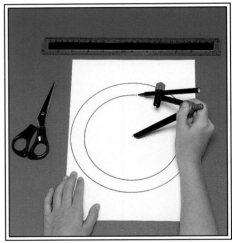

1 Draw a circle with a diameter of 4in. on the piece of white card stock. Draw three circles inside, each with a diameter 1⅛in. smaller than the last. Cut out the largest circle.

Inside the drive

A typical hard drive consists of a stack of thin disks, called a platter. The upper surface of each disk is coated with tiny magnetic particles, and each disk has its own read/write head on a movable arm. When storing and reading information, the disks spin at very high speeds (up to 100 revolutions a second).

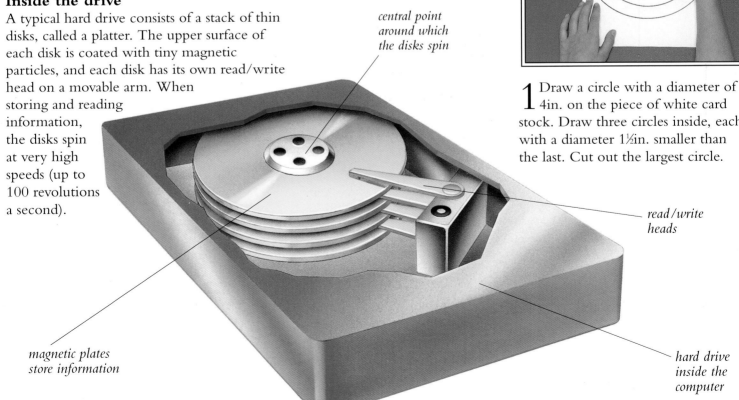

central point around which the disks spin

read/write heads

magnetic plates store information

hard drive inside the computer

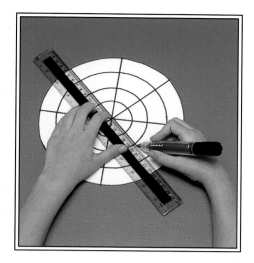

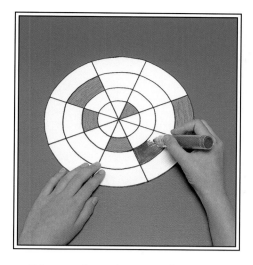

2 Position a ruler at the center of the circle where the compass point has made a hole. Draw four lines through the middle to divide the circle into eight equal parts.

3 Use a red marker to color in six or seven sections as shown above. Leave the remaining sections white. The white areas represent full disk space. Red areas are empty disk space.

4 Attach some reusable adhesive to the rim of a plastic cup. Then turn it upside down on a smooth surface. Press it down gently to make sure it is secure.

5 Push the tack through the middle of the colored disk and into the bottom of the cup, making sure that the disk can move around the pin. Scatter some paper clips on the surface. Hold the magnet under the disk. Move it around the disk.

6 The paper clips will move around the disk surface of the disk, too, and will all line up in a section of the disk. This is what happens to the magnetic particles on a hard disk when an electric current is passed through them by the read/write head. In a computer, the way the magnetic particles line up is a record of the data stored on the hard disk.

7 Remove the paper clips from the disk. Spin the disk clockwise with one hand and with a finger of the other touch areas of the disk. If you stop the disk on a white part you have found data. If you stop on a red section you have found empty disk space.

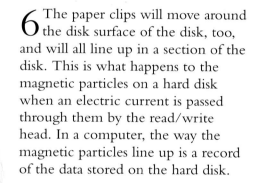

COMPUTER SOFTWARE

Linux
If you see this picture of a penguin when you are using a computer, then you know the computer is running an operating system called Linux.

SOFTWARE is a means of carrying a series of instructions that controls what computers do. There are two different types—systems software and applications software.

The basic systems software that controls the computer and makes it possible for us to use it is called the OS, or operating system. It includes instructions that manage the computer's memory, organize files and control devices such as scanners, printers and external storage drives. The operating system you have will depend on the type of computer you have. The most common is Microsoft Windows, which is used to operate most PCs. Apple Macintosh computers work using the Mac OS. Linux is another operating system that will run on both Macs and PCs. The operating system runs in the background all the time that the computer is on.

Applications software includes programs that allow the computer to perform specific tasks. It runs on top of the operating system. Common applications software includes word-processing packages such as Microsoft Word, graphics applications such as Adobe Photoshop, and also games such as Tomb Raider.

The Mac start-up screen
If you see this picture when you start up a computer, then you know it is an Apple Macintosh computer running a version of the Mac operating system.

Applications software
When you click on the Microsoft Word icon on your computer, a start-up screen appears on the monitor. Microsoft Word comes in many different languages so that people all over the world can use the application. The ones pictured are: Arabic (top left), German (bottom left), French (top right) and Spanish (bottom right). The start-up screen lets you interact with the computer. You can tell the computer what you want to do by clicking on various parts of the screen. Microsoft Word is an example of applications software, which is a set of instructions that allows you to carry out different tasks on your computer. Microsoft Word allows you to perform word-processing tasks such as writing a letter or a story.

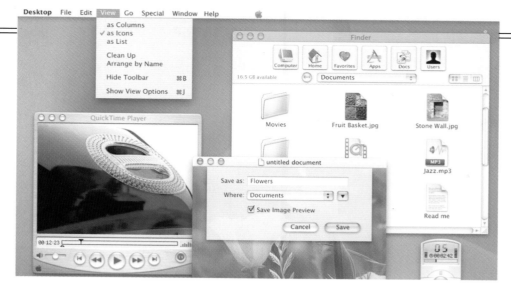

The Mac desktop

When an Apple Macintosh computer is switched on, the Mac operating system will automatically boot up. The desktop then appears on the monitor. The desktop is the starting point for doing tasks on the computer, and there are a number of different options you can choose from. The white bar at the top of the desktop is called the Menu Bar. If you hold down the mouse button on one of the words in the Menu Bar, a drop-down menu appears. If you highlight View, for example, you can change the way your desktop appears on the screen.

Using icons

Simple pictures, called icons, appear on the desktop to represent different jobs that the computer can do. You click on them to access files or to perform tasks. Icons are easy to recognize and help you to work easily. For example, Folder icons are where you keep your work. You can name the different folders so that you can find different files easily. The Hard Disk icon represents the main disk drive built into the computer. It stores the Operating System software, applications software and your work. The Recycle Bin on a PC and the Wastebasket on a Mac are where you put the files you do not want any more before you delete them for good. As long as they stay in the Wastebasket, you can take them out again if you change your mind.

Signpost icons

Each application software has a unique icon. When you double click on the icon with a mouse, the application opens so that you can use it. There are many different kinds of applications software. Word-processing software allows you to type and arrange text. Graphics software allows you to create images or manipulate old ones to improve them or turn them into a new picture. Internet browsers and e-mail software are essential if you want to use either facility. The icons above represent a range of different software.

Drop-downs and pop-ups

Most software works using drop-down and pop-up menus. When you click with your mouse on a word on

the monitor screen, you often find that a menu either drops down or pops up on screen and offers you a number of choices. Move the cursor to the one you want to select and click on it to perform the task you want.

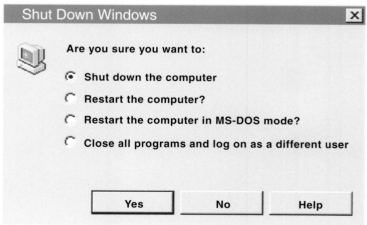

Dialogue boxes

When the computer needs to ask you a question, a window appears on the screen. If you are not sure what to do, there is a Help option, where you can look up information.

MOUSE CARE AND MOUSE PAD

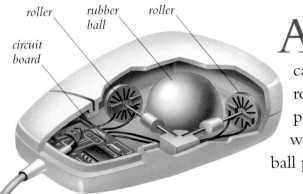

circuit board

roller

rubber ball

roller

A MOUSE is a device that allows you to interact with your computer. It moves the cursor on the screen, so that you can select different options. A rubber ball inside the mouse rolls like a wheel so the mouse can move over a special mouse pad. The ball then pushes against electrical contact points, which send signals to your computer. Unfortunately, the rubber ball picks up dust and dirt from the mouse pad, which then sticks to the contact points.

As more dirt accumulates, it becomes more difficult to move the cursor where you want it to go. The project on this page shows you how to clean your mouse.

Mouse pads are made from a spongy material that provides a good surface for the mouse to move around on. There are lots of fun designs, but you can make your own one if you like. The project on the opposite page shows you how.

Inside the mouse

Tiny circuits inside the mouse convert the movement of the rubber ball into electrical signals. The contact points are set on rollers in front of the mouse and to one side.

HOW TO CLEAN YOUR MOUSE

You will need:
rubbing alcohol, cotton swabs.

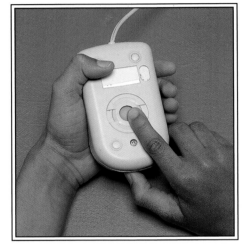

1 Hold the mouse upside down in one hand. Use the other hand to remove the cover around the ball. There are usually arrows on the mouse to show you how.

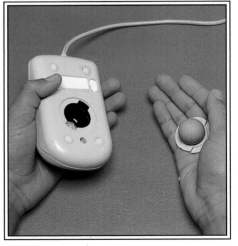

2 When the cover is loose, place the palm of your hand over the bottom of the mouse and turn it back the right way. The ball will fall out into your hand.

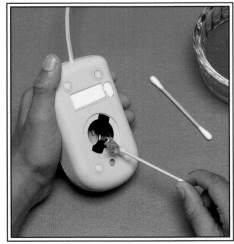

3 Moisten a cotton swab with rubbing alcohol and use it to clean the inside of the mouse. Most dirt sticks to the contact points, so be sure to clean these thoroughly.

4 You can wipe the ball clean as well if you like. When it is clean, place the ball back inside the mouse. Reposition the cover. Now your mouse should work better.

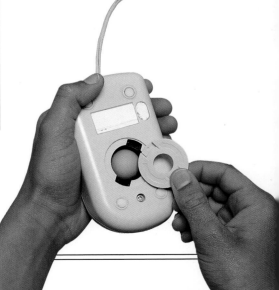

MAKE A MOUSE PAD

You will need:
computer and printer, heat-transfer
printing paper (available from a computer store),
plain mouse pad, pencil, ruler, scissors, iron.

1 Open up a colorful picture file from the clip-art folder. Measure the mouse pad and adjust the height and width of the picture (using the Measurements tool bar) so that it will fit on the pad. The image will be reversed when it is on the mouse pad, so don't choose a picture that has any writing on it.

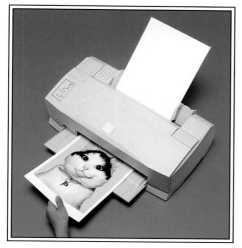

2 Put a piece of heat-transfer paper into the paper tray of your printer. Print the picture onto the coated side of the paper.

3 Place the pad over the printed picture and draw around the edge of the pad with a pencil. Carefully cut around the pencil marks.

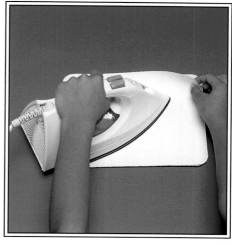

4 Look at the instructions given with the heat-transfer paper and set the iron to the right temperature. Put the print face side down on the top side of the pad and iron over it.

5 While the transfer paper is still warm, carefully peel off the backing paper to reveal your image. Let the mouse pad cool down for a few minutes.

6 It will take about 30 minutes for the mouse pad to cool before you can use it. The surface of mouse pads is designed to let the mouse run smoothly over them, but also to provide enough grip for the rubber ball to move. You could make a whole selection of mouse pads with different pictures on them—one for every day of the week.

WORKING WITH WORDS

WORD-PROCESSING applications are designed for working with text, such as a letter, and are widely used in offices and at home. They allow you to edit (change) the words you write at any time and even add pictures, too. If you want, you can stop your work for a while, store it on the computer's hard disk and return to finish it later. The final document can be printed on paper.

Word-processing applications can do some amazing things. You can move words around, copy words from one document to another and change the size and style of the letters very easily. It is even possible to check your spelling and grammar. Before word-processing applications were invented, people could write letters and documents on a typewriter. However, the time and trouble saved by using word-processing applications means that typewriters are rarely used today.

Typewriter trouble
An old-fashioned typewriter from the late 1800s could produce quicker and neater text than handwriting. However, mistakes had to be erased or painted over. The typist also had only one choice of type size and style.

News reporters
It would be hard to find a modern office that does not use computers in some way. Most of the workers in this CNN newsroom use a computer to do their work. The reporters use a word-processing application to type their reports, which makes it very easy to change any mistakes, add extra text or check the spelling and grammar. The most common word-processing applications are Microsoft Word for PCs and AppleWorks for Macs.

Fun with fonts

A typeface, or font, is a style of lettering. There are hundreds of fonts, and each one has a name that was thought up by the person who designed it. Some are installed on your computer when you buy it. These are called the system fonts. Others can be bought on a disk and loaded onto the computer's hard drive. You can put different fonts in the same document by choosing from the menu bar.

Helvetica
Times
Giddyup
Chicago

Text alignment

Words need to start and end somewhere specific to look neat on the page. Alignment makes words line up to the left or right margin or line up with the center of the page. You can change the alignment of a selected paragraph or sentence by checking one of three boxes (right, left or center) in the main tool bar.

You can also make the text spread out evenly between the left and the right margins, which is called justification. This paragraph is justified.

plain

bold

italic

<u>underline</u>

outline

Styling the type

Styling means changing the appearance of a font. Most fonts come in a set that contains a plain font and its alternatives. The alternatives are **bold**, which is a heavy type, *italic*, which is sloping, and ***bold italic***, which is both heavy and sloping. However, you can change the format of any font by checking a box in the tool bar. Here, you can underline fonts, outline them and even put shadows on them. You can also make the typeface a different color if you want, although you will only be able to print this if you have a color printer.

Alignment is making words line up to the left, center or right of the page.

This text is aligned or ranged LEFT.

Font size

You can choose how big your type appears by changing its point size. Points are measurement units that are smaller than ⅛th of an inch. This is 11.5 point, but you can see some different sizes on the right.

14 point

24 point

44 point

64 point

Alignment is making words line up to the left, center or right.

This text is aligned CENTER.

selected text

Selecting text

To delete words, copy them, align them or style them to change their appearance, you first have to select the text. To do this, move your cursor to the beginning of the words you want to change. Click with your mouse. You will see the insertion point appear. Drag your mouse across the words. They will become highlighted with a color. You can now edit them as you wish.

Alignment is making words line up to the left, center or right.

This text is aligned or ranged RIGHT.

MY LETTERHEAD

YOU can design a personal letterhead to use whenever you write a letter. As well as including your name and address, you can also add pictures. To design your letterhead, you will need word-processing application software such as AppleWorks or Microsoft Word, but any kind of word-processing software will do. You will also need a printer to print the finished design.

To illustrate the letterhead, you can use a photograph or an existing picture from a clip-art collection on disk. You can even draw and paint your own, using a graphics application if you have one. You will be amazed at the professional-looking results that can be achieved in a short amount of time.

THOMAS

STEPHANIE

Your personal logo

Companies and organizations all over the world have their own logo (badge), which identifies them. The logo might include a picture, a name designed in a certain typeface, and a color. You could design your own logo for your letterhead, using some of these ideas.

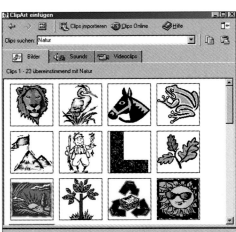

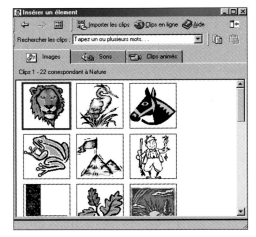

Clip art

Collections of images that come on disks are known as clip art. The different language versions shown in this picture of Microsoft Word clip art are: Hebrew (top left), German (bottom left), French (top right) and Spanish (bottom right). You can buy clip-art disks but some come free with computer magazines. Most office software includes clip-art collections. You can also download images from Internet sites to build up your own collection. Images are usually arranged into categories, such as animals or sports. To illustrate a word-processing document, you need to import the picture file from where it is stored, such as your computer's hard disk or a CD-ROM.

MAKE YOUR OWN LETTERHEAD

You will need:
computer with a word-processing application, printer, paper.

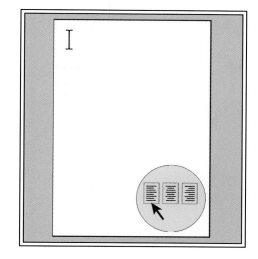

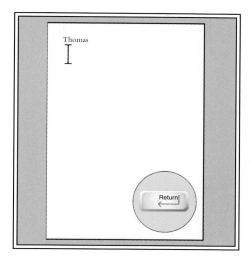

1 Open a new document. Set the size of your paper to 8½ × 11in. Click on the page and look for the insertion point. This is where your writing will go when you start to type.

2 Type in your name. Press the Return key when you want to go to a new line. You can choose a different font and change its size and color if you like.

3 When you have finished typing your address, place the insertion point where you want the picture to be. Drop in the picture file using the appropriate command on your computer.

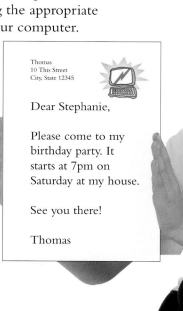

Thomas
10 This Street
City, State 12345

Dear Stephanie,

Please come to my birthday party. It starts at 7pm on Saturday at my house.

See you there!

Thomas

4 Try arranging the words and pictures in different ways. When you are happy with your design, save the document as "My letterhead" in your documents folder.

5 When you have finished writing your first letter, save it under a different name, such as "Letter 1." This means you can keep the original version of your letterhead to use again. Finally print a copy of your letter from your printer.

HOME OFFICE

MANY people keep records of useful information on their computer. They might list people's names and telephone numbers or record what needs to be done each day, just like a computerized diary. Office software, such as Microsoft Office, can be used for this purpose. As its name suggests, office software is mostly used by businesses, but it can be used by anyone.

For instance, you may want to store the names and addresses of all your closest friends. You would use a database program to do this. Databases allow you to store lots of information, which can be easily accessed and updated. Libraries use databases to store information about all the books they have. Information about your allowance can be recorded by using a spreadsheet program, which can perform all kinds of automatic calculations. Spreadsheets can add and subtract, converting dollars to pounds, for example, with the data they contain. You can also plot graphs and charts to show the information in a visual way.

Organizing your life

Some computers have an appointments diary, or personal organizer, as part of the office software. Some organizers can even remind you that you have an appointment by sounding an alarm.

Address book

Databases are used to keep records of data such as names, addresses, telephone numbers and e-mail addresses. They help you find and use the stored information easily. Databases can sort the information in different ways, such as in alphabetical or numerical order. Most office software contains a database application.

NAME	ADDRESS	PHONE	E-MAIL
Lucy	4 Big Street	555 1234	lucy@
James	23 Long Road	555 4567	james@
Poppy	14 Short Way	555 7890	poppy@

CANTEEN FOOD	January	February	March	Total of types
Pizzas	220	360	209	789
Pasta	170	238	273	681
Burgers	186	92	156	434
Fish	26	15	29	70
Total meals a month	602	705	667	

Counting and calculating

A spreadsheet is a display of numerical information that does automatic calculations. A spreadsheet is made up of lots of little boxes called cells. The size of the cells can be changed to fit the information—either words or numbers—entered. Spreadsheet software can work out calculations on numbers contained in the spreadsheet. For example, each column can be added up. If you change one number, the total appears automatically at the bottom of the column. In this way, people can easily keep up-to-date records of their finances.

Comparing information

Sometimes it is useful to show numerical information visually to help you understand it more easily. Many spreadsheet applications can automatically draw pie charts or graphs to represent information in an accessible way. The pie chart on the right shows how much of each kind of food is being eaten during school mealtimes. The total number of meals is represented by the circle. Each section, or pie, represents the different sorts of meals that are being eaten. From the chart, it is possible to see in an instant that pizzas are the most popular food by far and that fish is chosen the least. You can also see that about a quarter of the total number of meals eaten are burgers.

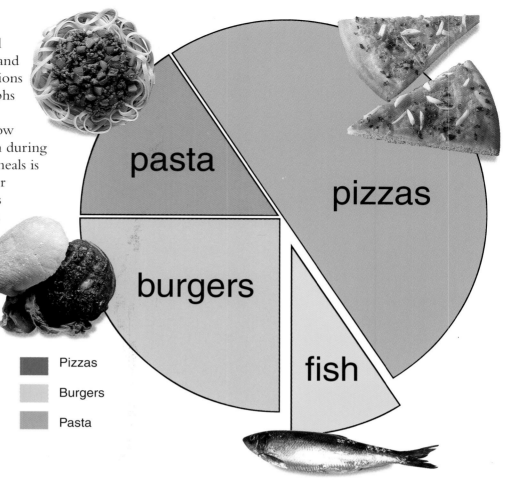

pasta

pizzas

burgers

fish

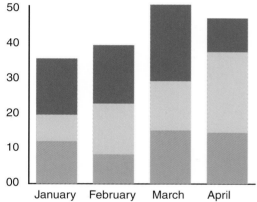

Pizzas

Burgers

Pasta

Column graphs

Spreadsheet packages can draw graphs to show how two different things, called variables, are related to one another. A common variable is time (days, weeks or months), which is always plotted horizontally, from left to right. Other variables, such as the type of food being eaten, can be plotted vertically from bottom to top. By reading the two sets of information on the graph above, you can see exactly how much of each kind of food was eaten in four given months of the year. There are two main types of graph—a column graph (above) and a line graph (above right). These graphs are two different ways of representing the same information.

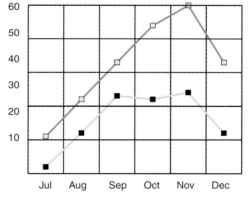

Pizzas

Pasta

Line graphs

As in the column graph, time is shown horizontally, and another variable, such as food being eaten, is show vertically. Each line represents one type of information, in this case pizzas or pasta. It is easy to see that more pizzas are being eaten than pasta in every month.

timetable	9:00	10:00	11:00	12:00	1:00	2:00	3:00
MONDAY	math	gym	science	lunch	computing	english	art
TUESDAY	music	english	math	lunch	science	history	geography
WEDNESDAY	history	english	geography	lunch	english	gym	gym
THURSDAY	english	music	art	lunch	math	geography	history
FRIDAY	science	computing	math	lunch	music	art	english

Make a timetable

You could make your own chart to remind you of your daily schedule or important events. Using a spreadsheet program, make a chart for your school timetable. Type in the days in a vertical column on the left and the hours along the top line. Then fill in the corresponding activities.

27

DESKTOP PUBLISHING

DESKTOP publishing (DTP) is the term given to computer applications that allow words and images to be arranged together on a page. Most books and magazines are designed using desktop publishing software, because writing, typesetting (arranging words on a page) and illustration can all be done in one place and sometimes even by the same person. This has made the publishing process easier than ever before.

Today, anyone with a computer and the necessary software can create his or her own magazine or newspaper. Each different part of the publication—the words, photographs and illustrations—is prepared separately. Then the software brings all the elements together. Desktop publishing software is fairly easy to use. Changes to the layout of a page, such as moving an illustration or inserting an extra paragraph into a story, can be done at any point during the process. Today, millions of books and magazines are created in such a way that they can even be published on the Internet.

From words to a page
Journalists and authors may make written notes or tape record their work and then type it up using a word-processing application such as Microsoft Word. They can e-mail their work to the newspaper or publishing office where it can be worked on and made into pages.

Instant pictures
Digital cameras capture still images electronically and do not use photographic film. The photographs are stored on a disk and can be loaded directly on to a computer, missing out the expensive and time-consuming film-processing stage. The images can then be imported straight into the pages of the document.

Making the layout
All pages in newspapers, books and magazines are arranged on a basic grid like the one on the right, because it makes the pages neat and easy to read. The first stage in making a page is to design a blank grid or to use one that already exists. A grid shows the size of the page and the area in which the text and the pictures will fit. It might also show where the text and the pictures line up. Then the designer can start to work on each individual page. He or she will import (place) the pictures into boxes on the page where they look best.

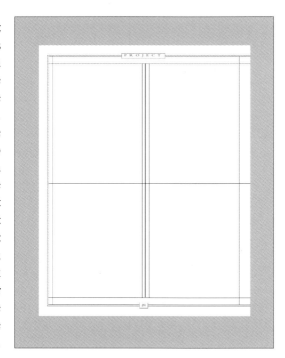

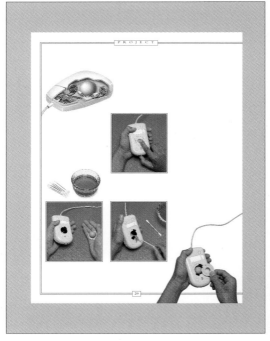

The publishing process

A book designer works on the illustrations before importing them into the pages. Before computers were invented, it took many different processes and many more people to arrive at a stage where a book or newspaper was finished. Today, the process is more straightforward and involves fewer people. This is especially important for newspapers, because they have to get the latest news to their readers as quickly as possible.

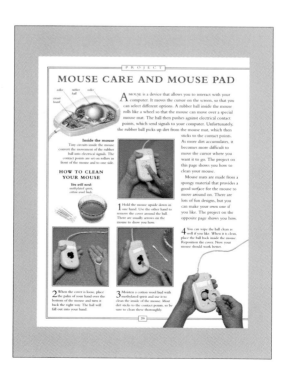

The finished page

The designer imports the text that goes with the pictures. He or she tries out different layouts until a good design has been found. The editor then checks the text and makes sure it matches the pictures, and that the blocks of text are not too long or too short. When the designer and the editor are both happy that the page is correct, it can go off to be printed and published. Desktop publishing applications make it easy to write, design and print your own pages, with a professional look. You can create posters, invitations or newsletters—any document that combines words and pictures.

FACT BOX

• Every publication, from a newspaper to a book, has a house style that distinguishes it from other publications.

• Desktop publishing applications can be used to set up a template in which the text and pictures follow a house style. The Fact Box you are reading now is written in a style that is the same throughout this book. Compare it with one on another page. You will see that the font is always the same size and the background is always the same color.

• QuarkXPress is the most popular page-layout software. Other applications include InDEsign and Publisher.

DAILY NEWS

A LOT of thought goes into designing the pages of a book or newspaper. First, the contents of the page are carefully planned on paper. Then, the layout designer arranges the words and pictures using a professional page-layout application such as QuarkXPress. The good thing about using a computer to do this kind of work is that it can be changed with little effort. This project shows you how to make a magazine page using your own computer. If you do not have a page-layout program, word-processing applications, such as Microsoft Word or AppleWorks, can be used instead.

Type an article
The first step in making any publication is to decide what you want to write about. You could gather together some stories and poems from your friends, or you could type some articles about news and events. Arrange them into an order that would make sense if someone was reading them all together on a page.

Scan some pictures
You will also need some pictures for your publication. If you have a scanner, scan in all the pictures and save them in a separate folder. If you do not have one of your own, use the scanner at school. When you have scanned all the images, copy them onto a removable disk, take the disk home and copy all the files onto your hard drive.

EDITOR FOR A DAY

You will need: computer with a desktop publishing application or a word-processing application such as Microsoft Word, printer, paper.

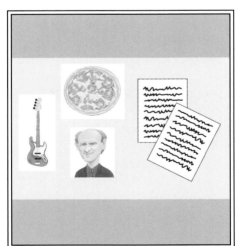

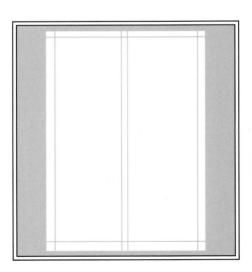

1 Collect all the items you want to put on your page. This will enable you to work out how much space you will need to fit all the words and pictures onto your page.

2 Open a document and set the document size to 8½ × 11in. Set a 1½-in. margin around the edge of your page. Position two guide lines in the center of the page, about ¾in. apart.

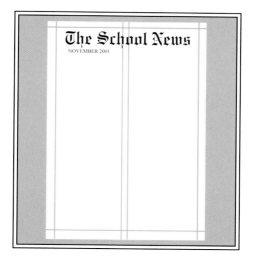

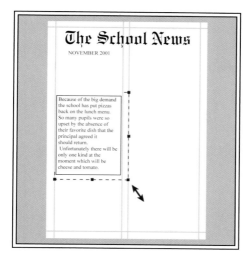

3 Make a text box at the top of the page. Type in a title. Increase the point size to make the words bigger. Make a smaller text box to add other header information.

4 Make another text box in the first column. Set the point size to 12 and type your story. You can resize the text box by dragging the corner points with the cursor.

5 Make a picture box and import your picture. You can resize the box by dragging the corner points to fit the column. Position the picture near the text box.

6 Add more pictures and words until the page is full. The boxes can be moved around or resized to fit everything on the page. If you have too many things to fit on one page, make another page.

7 Once you are happy with the layout, print out as many copies as you need and give them to your family and friends.

Pictures on screen

A layout designer in a newspaper office scans some images onto his computer. He will then use them to make up part of the article he is laying out on the page.

A SPLASH OF COLOR

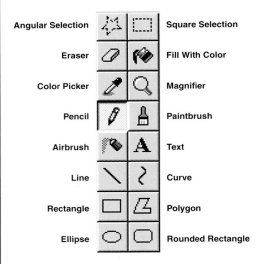

Angular Selection			Square Selection
Eraser			Fill With Color
Color Picker			Magnifier
Pencil			Paintbrush
Airbrush			Text
Line			Curve
Rectangle			Polygon
Ellipse			Rounded Rectangle

The tools palette

The Toolbar contains digital versions of real art tools such as a pencil, an airbrush and an eraser. Clicking on these icons will activate them. The Toolbar also gives you the option of drawing specific shapes, such as circles, and styles of lines. You can use a combination of all these effects on one illustration.

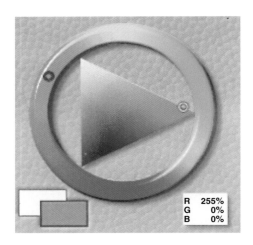

Choosing color

Painting software contains palettes of different colors from which you can select and mix. Each color has a number equivalent on the Red-Green-Blue (RGB) scale. By typing in varying percentages of red, green and blue, you can mix different colors. You can save these numbers on the color palette and use the same shade again.

MANY special visual effects are possible with computers that would be very difficult to do by hand. Graphics applications have the advantage that if mistakes are made, it is very easy to correct them. For example, all graphics applications have an Eraser tool, which can instantly remove something you don't like. As well as the normal drawing and painting tools, other tools can be used to create special effects. The Airbrush tool creates a fine spray effect to paint colors on your picture. There is a variety of backgrounds to give the final picture a different appearance. Most computers come with basic painting and drawing software. For a wide range of special finishing touches, such as gradient fills and airbrush effects, advanced software such as Painter and Microsoft Paint is available.

Multiple techniques

Most painting software enables you to create many different effects. Some give brush strokes of varied thickness, and others create airbrush effects to add to your work. Try all the different tools. The four segments of this apple were drawn using (clockwise from top left): a colored pencil, an airbrush, different brush strokes, chalk and wax crayon textures.

Brush strokes

Most applications provide a selection of different tools, such as brushes, pens, crayons and pencils, to choose from. You can experiment with crayon and chalk textures for graffiti styles, soft pencils and airbrushes for shading, washes for backgrounds and even watercolors and oil paint effects to recreate more classic works of art. You do not have to be a brilliant artist to draw and paint pictures on a computer, because the software is designed to be easy to use. Most of the effects can be created in just one click of a mouse.

Looking closer

When an image is magnified, you can see that it is made up of individual blocks of color that, in turn, consist of thousands of tiny dots of light called pixels (short for picture elements). Just like words, pictures are stored in the computer as binary code.

Basic shapes

Basic shapes, such as circles and squares, can be made by selecting them from the Toolbar. Another tool, called the Polygon tool, lets you draw your own shapes. You can fill the shapes with color.

Gradient fills

A gradient fill is a graduated blend between two or more colors or tints of the same color. You can achieve smooth color and tonal transitions when filling images with the Gradient tool.

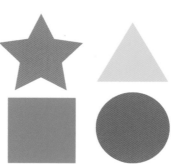

Photo painting

Painting software allows you to work with photographs you may have already scanned and saved on your computer's hard disk. Draw in a hat, some glasses and a moustache to a picture of your face to make a fun picture.

COMPUTER GRAPHICS

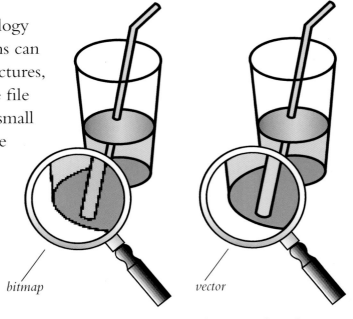

Artworks that are created using computer technology are called computer graphics. Graphics applications can be used to create new pictures or to change existing pictures, such as photographs, that are already stored as a picture file on a computer. Pictures are displayed on the screen as small dots of color called pixels. The computer registers these tiny bits of information as binary code. Whenever you change a picture by moving it, cutting parts out or adding new parts, the computer makes a note of how the pixels have been changed and revises the binary code to record what you have done. Once people used to say that a camera never lies. Today, however, nearly all the photographs used in advertisements have been altered by computers in some way.

Computer graphics can range from simple photographic images to the complex and extremely realistic drawings used in virtual reality, the process by which a computer is used to create an artificial place that appears real, such as in a flight simulator.

bitmap *vector*

The make-up of an image

Computer graphics are either bitmap images or vector graphics. Photographs and painted effects are bitmaps. Each pixel that makes up a bitmap is given a specific color and location by the computer. Vector graphics are used a lot for line drawings. In these, the computer records each shape and color as a code. The difference is most apparent when the images are enlarged. Bitmaps develop jagged edges, but vector graphics stay smooth at any size.

Funny faces

Some weird and wonderful effects can be created by applying different filters to a photograph. A filter is a mathematical formula that the computer uses to distort a picture. Most computer graphics applications have filters built into them. Different filters move pixels around in different ways. Some filters do simple things such as sharpening or blurring an image. Others can distort a picture to add an unusual texture or make color changes.

Coming to life

Animation is the process by which pictures are made to move around. Animation is done by putting together hundreds of pictures, each one showing a small change in movement. The pictures that make up an animation can either be flat (two-dimensional) or three-dimensional (appear to have depth). Before computers, animations were done by hand. Computers can fill in the gaps between movements and reduce the number of pictures that need to be drawn.

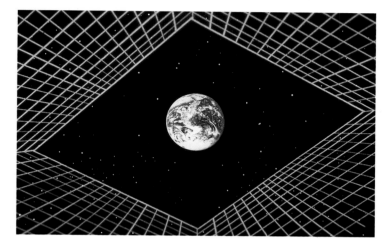

Clear or fuzzy?

The number of pixels that make up an image is known as the resolution, which is usually measured as the total number of pixels in a square inch. The more pixels, the clearer the image. For example, the two pictures above are the same, but the one on the left has a higher resolution.

Creating the image

Three-dimensional graphics have to be modeled in the same way as sculptures. Firstly, a simple shape, called the wireframe, is made of lines. The wireframe above forms a tunnel looking down at Earth. It will be covered with texture and color to give it a realistic appearance.

Altered images

Graphics software, such as Adobe Photoshop and Microsoft Paint, allow you to do amazing things with images. For example, you can copy parts of one photograph and put them on another to create an unusual or unreal image. In the picture on the left, the fish have been copied from one photograph and then positioned on the picture of Concorde flying in the sky. Using graphics software, you can also clean marks or scratches on a photographic image, change its size, brightness, resolution and color and then print it out. Some graphics software allows you to select and remove areas of a picture or paint over them with other parts of the same image. So you could create a photograph of yourself in a famous city where you have never been.

CREATE A PHOTO POSTER

Changing photographs is easy on a computer. You can erase parts that you do not want, paint in new areas, such as a background, or copy and move parts of the picture around. This project uses an application, such as Adobe Photoshop or Paint Shop Pro, that enables you to open picture files and then change them. Collect some photographs you find around the house, such as pictures of your family and friends. Even passport-size photographs will do. All the changes you make are done on a picture file on the computer, so you can be as experimental as you like without worrying about ruining the original photograph. You will need to use a scanner unless you have your photos on a disk or stored in the computer already. A scanner transfers the photograph on to your computer as a picture file.

Caricatures
A caricature of the British pop group the Spice Girls has been drawn using computer graphics software. You could get together with some of your friends, take photos of each other and then scan them on to your computer's hard disk. Alter the photos using a graphics application such as Painter.

MAKING YOUR OWN PHOTO POSTER

You will need: photographs, computer with a scanner, printer and a computer-graphics application.

1 Collect some pictures of your friends. Use the scanner to transfer them on to your computer. Save each picture file in a new folder named "Photos of my friends."

2 Start your graphics application. Open a new document and make a page 8in. wide and 8in. high. Fill it with a colored background. Save the document as "My friends."

3 Open a picture file. Click on the picture and copy it. Click on your new document and paste the picture, dragging it into place with your mouse. Do the same with all the picture files.

4 Select the background color from the color palette. Select a brush and paint out the background behind the faces. Use a smaller brush around the edges of the picture.

5 Select the Text tool from the tools palette. Click where you want the words to start and type them in. Choose a bold typeface and a color that shows up well on the background.

Computer art

There are lots of ways that people create art using computer technology. One of the most amazing effects can be produced by using fractals (short for fractal dimension). Fractals are complex shapes often found in nature. Computer programs create fractal images using complex mathematical formulas. By manipulating the formulas, artists can generate stunning and intricate patterns, such as this one on the right.

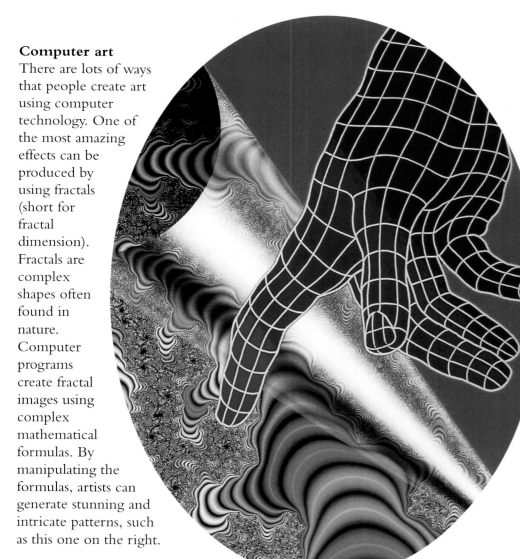

6 Once you are happy with your design, save the document onto your computer's hard disk. You can then print it out poster-size. Select the Print menu from the menu bar, adjust the printer setting to fit your poster on the paper and press Print.

GAME FOR A LAUGH

COMPUTER games are the second biggest use of computers after word-processing. The computers people use to play games come in different forms. The largest are arcade machines that have big screens, loud sound effects and special controls such as steering wheels and guns. However, you can play games at home on computers such as GameBoy, PlayStation, Nintendo 64, Dreamcast, or even on your desktop computer. The most popular computer games are probably the interactive games, in which the player can control what happens on screen.

Some games can be played using the mouse and keyboard. Other games use special devices, such as a joystick or gamepad, to control parts of the game. These allow easy and fast control of the graphics in action games, when you need to react quickly to what you see on screen. Today's computer games feature high-speed, colorful, three-dimensional graphics, as well as realistic visual and sound effects.

GameBoy

One of the most popular game computers is the hand-held GameBoy. The games are supplied on cartridges, which slot into the back of the Game Boy. There are hundreds of different games to choose from.

Sport for all

Today, you can play just about every type of sport on a computer. There are football, car racing and snowboarding games, to name a few. Some sports games are called simulations, because they re-create the sport in lifelike way. In this skiing simulation, the player holds poles and stands on moving platforms, which simulate skis. The movements of his arms and legs are interpreted by sensors on the computer and then re-created on the computer screen.

Console computers

The PlayStation and Nintendo 64 are called console computers, which means they need to be connected to a television to display pictures. The game is controlled using a gamepad, which consists of two joysticks and lots of buttons. Console computers can now connect to the Internet so people from all over the world can play against each other.

Be a pilot

Simulation games let you imitate real-life situations that you control through the computer. In the flight simulator shown on the left, you can get an idea of what it is like to fly a civil aircraft to destinations all over the world. Others involve battles with military aircraft.

Rule the world

In strategy games, the player takes on the role of a government or ruler and must follow a set of objectives to create a successful city or civilization. Examples of strategy games include Alpha Centauri, Civilization, Settlers, Sim City and Tiberian Sun. In Sim City, the player becomes the mayor of a futuristic city. The people who live there want it all—industry and clean air, convenient housing and open space, low taxes and low crime rates. Can you strike a balance and turn your city into a thriving metropolis? Other strategy games allow you to create people with different personalities. You can put them in houses and make them act out real-life situations.

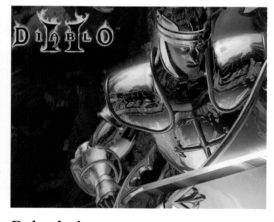

Spin and play

People watch while a girl spins around and upside down in an R–360 video game. The player is strapped into a small cockpit. She uses a joystick to control a jet fighter during a virtual dog-fight (fight between two planes). The cockpit is enclosed in a gyroscope, which allows the cockpit to spin around in any direction, simulating the movement of a real jet fighter.

Role playing

Forget what it is like to be human and become a fantasy character in a role-playing game such as Diablo II. You can immerse yourself in a world of intrigue and adventure set in a forgotten land. Role-playing games such as Diablo have attractive graphics and are very easy to use.

DESIGNING GAMES

M ANY people are involved in designing a computer game, and it is a very time-consuming process. Graphic designers come up with lifelike pictures of characters, and computer animators make characters and objects move in a realistic way. When all the parts of a game are finished, people called computer programmers write a list of instructions, called a program, which the computer uses to make all the different parts of the game work together so you can play it. It is very difficult to learn how to program modern computers to play games.

If you like playing games, here is a spot-the-difference game that you can make using your computer and play anywhere. It can be created just by using photographs or by painting and drawing your own picture.

Central character

Many games have a central character for the players to identify with. This is one of the characters from the game Crash Team Racing.

GAMING AROUND

You will need: photographs, computer with a scanner, printer and a computer-graphics application.

Playtime

A boy plays games on his computer. At the side of the keyboard, there is a selection of floppy disks from which he can download different games. More and more people have their own computers at home. Although computers are useful tools and are fun to play with, it is important not to spend all your spare time using your computer. You should do other things as well, such as playing outdoor sports and talking or listening to music with your friends.

1 Choose some images to make into a picture. Before you begin, sketch out your picture as a guide. Scan each photograph and save them all on your computer's hard disk.

Computer chess

Chessmaster 7000 is a computerized version of the traditional board game, chess. Instead of playing with another person, however, the computer is your opponent. Before you start, you select the level of difficulty to match the standard of your play.

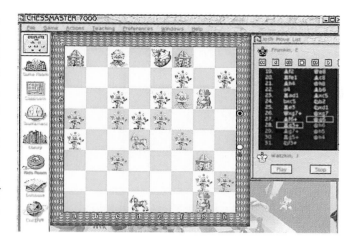

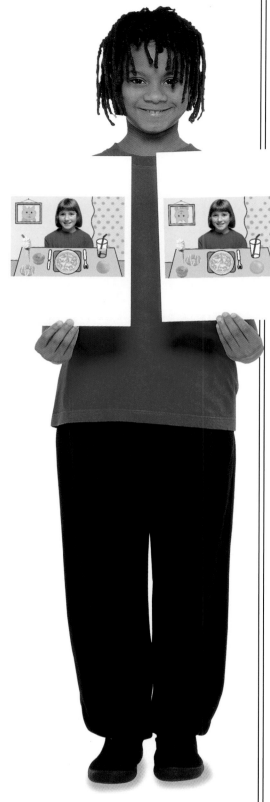

2 Open your graphics application. Then open a new document and save it as "Picture 1." Choose a background color and draw in the main areas of your picture.

3 Open one of the photograph files you scanned. Copy and paste it onto the main picture. Do the same for all the photograph files. You can draw and paint images if you like.

4 When you have completed your picture, save it as "Picture 1" again. Then select Save As from the File menu. Type "Picture 2" and save a second copy of the same picture.

5 Now you can change things on Picture 2. Change the color of something, change its size, move it to another place and remove or add things. Make about six changes.

6 Print out copies of both pictures, and ask a friend to spot the differences between the two. The more subtle you make the changes, the harder it will be for the person playing the game to spot them all. The person who spots all the differences the quickest is the winner.

MULTIMEDIA

MULTIMEDIA means bringing together different kinds of communication (media) such as text, photographs, moving pictures and sounds. Encyclopedias, especially, can be a lot of fun when they can let you hear the sound a bird makes or show you how a machine moves. Multimedia is used for teaching, games, giving information in public places, advertising, and accessing reference material. The multimedia user is given control over the information, which means he or she can make choices about how they move through the work and can select what is presented to them. This way of working with the information is called interaction. Click with a mouse on a picture or highlighted words to jump to other pages or bring special effects into play such as animations, sound or a video clip. Multimedia is commonly found on the Internet and reference CD-ROMs such as Microsoft's *Encarta* encyclopedia.

Home library

Reference books, such as encyclopedias and atlases, work well when translated into multimedia because they can show much more than flat, still, visual information. Video clips can show how machines or animals move or what people and places look like. Added sounds can reproduce people's voices or allow the music of a singer or composer to be heard. Multimedia reference publications can also link similar articles together.

Showing the way

Museums, airports, and other public places often have multimedia kiosks to give information to the public. They often use a technology called touch screen where viewers point to the item they want to know about with their finger instead of a mouse. Sensors detect changes in the electrical current on the screen, work out what area of the screen is being touched and then provide information related to the area of interest.

Learn a language

This boy is learning how to speak French on his home computer using a multimedia language package. Foreign language students can hear the language being spoken as well as having their own voice recorded and checked for the correct pronunciation. Interactive games and puzzles can test the student's understanding of a particular topic they have learned. Multimedia is an extremely useful tool in the classroom, because the students can work through the topic at their own speed. They can replay any information they are unsure about and can quickly cross-reference related areas by adding bookmarks and their own personal notes. Many school subjects are now being taught using multimedia CD packages.

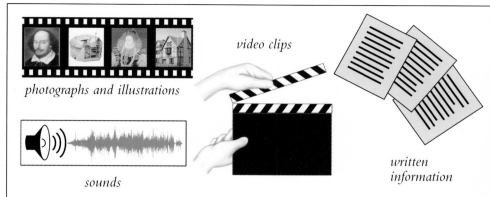

video clips

photographs and illustrations

sounds

written information

Making multimedia
There are many stages involved in making a multimedia product. First, how the product is going to look, what it will contain and how the parts will link together have to be worked out. When this has been decided, a team of researchers must find all the material, such as video clips, images, sounds and written information.

The final result
Once all the information has been gathered, the various media are linked using a special computer language. This is an electronic connection between media in the product, allowing the user to cross-reference between similar topics, pictures, animations or videos. At the same time, a team of software engineers will develop the "run-time engine," a computer application that coordinates and runs all the elements of the product. Once everything is in place, the product is tested extensively to identify any problems that may have cropped up during the production process.

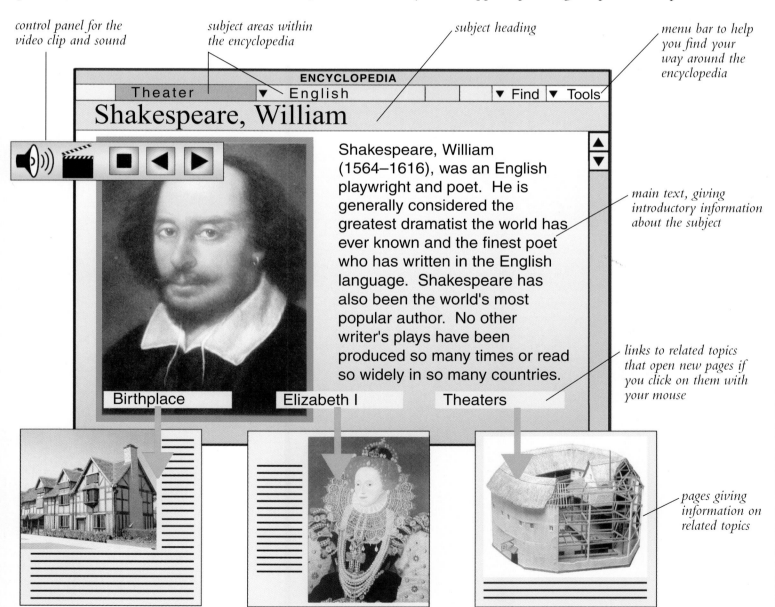

control panel for the video clip and sound

subject areas within the encyclopedia

subject heading

menu bar to help you find your way around the encyclopedia

main text, giving introductory information about the subject

links to related topics that open new pages if you click on them with your mouse

pages giving information on related topics

ENCYCLOPEDIA

Theater ▼ English ▼ Find ▼ Tools

Shakespeare, William

Shakespeare, William (1564–1616), was an English playwright and poet. He is generally considered the greatest dramatist the world has ever known and the finest poet who has written in the English language. Shakespeare has also been the world's most popular author. No other writer's plays have been produced so many times or read so widely in so many countries.

Birthplace

Elizabeth I

Theaters

VIRTUAL REALITY

COMPUTERS can create an artificial place and situation that looks very real indeed. The virtual world is actually made up of many different three-dimensional graphics, which together imitate the real world or create a very convincing one. The viewer can move around the virtual environment by using an input device such as a control pad, mouse or keyboard. As the viewer changes view or moves somewhere, the graphic on the screen changes to respond to the action of the viewer. There are two types of virtual reality (VR)—immersive and desktop. Immersive VR is extremely realistic and is most often used for arcade games and for scientific and business research. Desktop VR is less sophisticated and can be experienced on a home computer.

In another world

Immersive VR is so realistic that it makes viewers believe they are actually inside a different world. The user may have to wear a head-mounted display unit on his or her head. This is a helmet that has a computer screen inside. The screen displays the virtual environment. As the user's head turns, the display on the computer screen changes, just as in real life. The viewer can interact with the environment using a glove with sensors to detect hand movements.

Squash for one

A boy plays squash on a virtual reality court. As the ball comes towards him, he swings the racket. The computer senses his movements and plays the ball back to him. Virtual squash might be fun, but you would get more healthy exercise playing a real game of squash.

Drive safely

In this version of virtual reality, the image is projected on to a screen in front of the user. The screen fills the field of vision, so that the player actually feels as if he or she is driving along the road. Sensors attached to the car and to the driver's helmet detect the eye, arm and leg movements. This virtual reality situation is designed for developing a computerized warning system in cars that will alert the driver if he or she is about to do anything dangerous. Applications of this type are increasingly popular ways of training people in situations that would otherwise be too dangerous.

Virtual visitor

VR has been used to recreate the tomb of Nefertari, the wife of Pharaoh Ramses II of Egypt. The virtual visitor can walk through the burial chambers, which are decorated with murals and hieroglyphic writing. The viewer uses a trackball mouse to move around the burial chambers. This mouse has a rolling ball on top, which makes navigation smoother. Some even have an up and down facility so that the viewer can observe high and low viewpoints of his or her surroundings. This virtual reality is called desktop VR, because you can use a home computer to explore the environment. Although the effect is convincing, it is not as lifelike as immersive virtual reality. The controls available are less sophisticated, although headsets are now becoming available.

Fun and games

These people are playing a virtual reality game in an amusement park. The players are using their headsets to collect clues needed to solve a mystery in a virtual world. Games such as these allow players to interact with one another as they move around their environment.

Practice makes perfect

The cockpit of a flight simulator imitates all aspects of flight, including weather conditions and details of all the airports in the world. By imitating real flight, the pilot can make mistakes without putting real passengers in danger.

The future of virtual reality

The cybersphere is the next step in virtual reality technology. It allows the user to be totally immersed in a simulated world, not just via a headset. It is a large see-through ball made of interlocking plates and mounted on a cushion of air. Users can walk, run or jump, and a smaller ball connected to the large one detects these movements. In the future, this technology could be used in the military to train soldiers.

THE SOUND OF MUSIC

RECORDING and playing sounds and music is another task that a computer can do. You can play audio CDs or write, record and mix your own music. The sound that we hear—for example, from a musical instrument—travels to our ears through the air in waves, called sound waves. Computers can convert sound waves to electrical signals. These are subsequently converted into binary code, so that the computer can recognize them. When a microphone picks up sound waves, it passes them to an analogue-to-digital converter. This device converts sound waves to digital signs. The opposite conversion takes place when the computer plays music.

Sound files take up a lot of the computer's memory, but new technology, such as the MP3 system, can reduce the size of the files while keeping the quality of the sound. There are hundreds of web sites on the Internet where you can download MP3 files of your favorite music and store it on your own CDs. In the future, most of our music may come from the Internet in this way. In this project, you can find out how to make your own CD covers for music that you download.

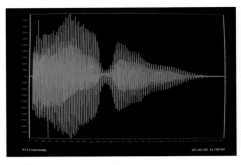

Voice recognition
Talking to a computer is not as strange as it might seem. Software can now analyze a person's voice patterns, making it possible to give a computer instructions without ever touching it. This software is very useful for people with disabilities.

MAKE A CD COVER

You will need: a selection of images, computer with a computer-graphics application, printer, scissors, CD case.

Sound studio
Digital sound recording has practically replaced analogue (tape) recording because the sound quality is so much better. Computers have made the job a whole lot easier, too. Applications called sequencers record tracks (different parts of a piece of music, such as guitar or drums). The sequencer records short sequences of the sound the instruments are producing at regular intervals. These are then translated into binary code so they can be stored in the computer.

1 Choose all the images you would like to use on your CD cover. Place them all in their own folder on your computer so that you will be able to find them easily.

2 Using your graphics application, draw a box that measures 5 × 5in. Use the ruler guides to help you get the right size. Start to create a design using the painting tools.

3 Bring in photographic images if you want to use them. Open the photo first, select it, and then use Copy and Paste to transfer it to your design. Add some text for the title.

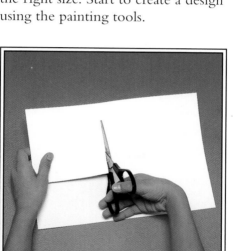

4 When you are happy with your design save it on your computer's hard disk. Print the final design out at 100 percent. Carefully cut out your print.

5 Slide the print into the CD case lid. You can also take out the removable plastic disc holder and make another design for the back and spine of the CD case.

Music maker
Some music software can actually make the sounds of musical instruments. They also write out the music as the notes are being played. The computer then records the sound and stores it so it can be played again.

6 If you have a CD writer and regularly download music from the Internet, you will not have a cover to make your CD stand out. It is easy to make your own covers using existing pictures and photos. Look in your clip-art folder to see if there are any images you can use. You can even draw and paint your own designs.

THE INTERNET AND E-MAIL

THE Internet is a global network that allows computers to exchange information. The first computer networks were developed in the 1960s, but the rapid explosion of the 1990s resulted from the rapid growth of personal computing and the improvement of the modem (modulator/demodulator). The Internet has many applications. Perhaps the most popular is electronic mail, or e-mail for short. Using e-mail, messages can be delivered to a computer user on the other side of the world in a matter of minutes. However, the most impressive application of the Internet is the World Wide Web (www). This allows a user to set up a computer document called a web page, look up other web pages, search for data using a search engine and download the latest software.

Sky high
Communications satellites are just one part of a vast system that enables data to be transmitted all over the world by the Internet.

Traffic jams
A computer graphic represents Internet traffic throughout the world. Each colored line represents the Internet traffic from a different country. For example, the United States is pink and the United Kingdom is dark blue. Internet traffic is set to increase as more and more people connect to the Internet.

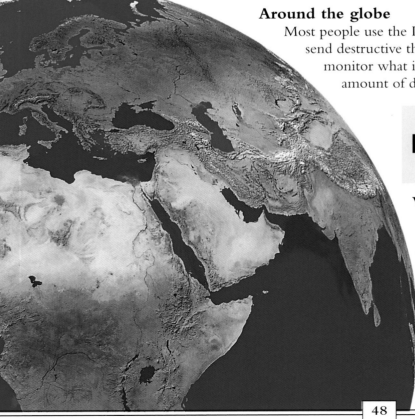

Around the globe
Most people use the Internet to send and receive useful data but some send destructive things, such as computer viruses. It is difficult to monitor what is being sent on the Internet, because a huge amount of data is sent all over the world each day.

mary@bigworld.com

What's in an address?
All e-mail addresses contain the @ symbol, which means "at." The part before the @ is called the user name, in this case "Mary." The part after the @ is called the domain name, which is the place where the user can be found. In this case, the domain name is "bigworld." The domain name is often followed by a code that tells you what type of site it is. For example, "com" means it is a commercial site. Many addresses also contain a code for the country, such as "uk" for the United Kingdom, "fr" for France and "au" for Australia.

Mailing electronic messages

E-mail software allows you to send and receive e-mails, write and edit messages, and store e-mail addresses in a contacts folder. To use e-mail on your own computer, you must be connected to the Internet, and a company known as an Internet Service Provider (ISP) allows you to do this. You also have to install a browser (software that lets you look at the Internet) on your computer.

Alternatively, you can use a service provided by an e-mail portal company, such as Hotmail and Yahoo! This service allows you to send and access your mail from any computer connected to the Internet.

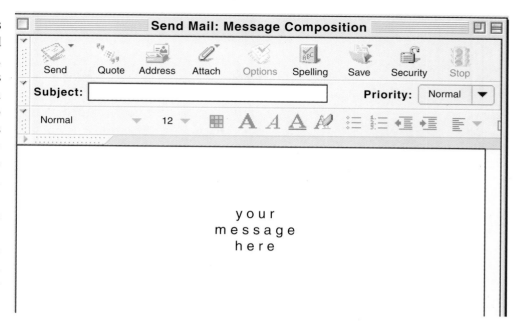

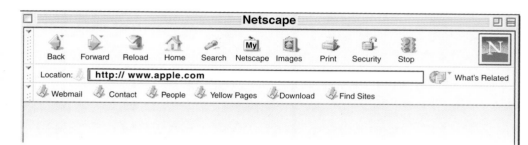

Internet browsers

Two well-known browsers are Internet Explorer and Netscape Navigator. Both have an e-mail facility built into them. When you start up your e-mail software, which is called logging on, messages that have been sent to you show up automatically on the screen.

Smileys

These little pictures are made up from combinations of keyboard punctuation marks, such as semi-colons, colons, dashes and parenthesis. Smileys are used by people in their e-mails to describe an expression or emotion that they want to communicate to the reader. They are used to represent faces. Look at them sideways to see the face. Here are some well-known smileys. Maybe you can think of some new ones.

:-)	happy	;-)	wink
:-(	sad	:-o	surprised
:-x	not speaking	/-o	bored
O:-)	angel	:-/	confused
;-(	crying	]:-[	angry
:-P	tongue out	:-D	laughing
:-*	clowning around		

Coffee and Internet

Internet cafes, or cybercafes, allow people who do not have a computer of their own to access the Internet. You can surf the Internet and look at different web sites while you have a cup of coffee or some lunch. Cybercafes are also ideal for people who travel a lot or are on holiday. However, they may become less popular when pocket-size personal computers that can connect to the Internet become available.

SEND AN E-POSTCARD

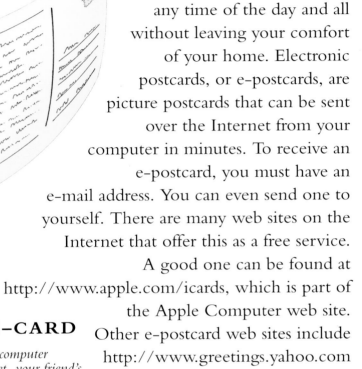

H AVE you ever missed an important birthday and found yourself rushing to catch the mail? This will never happen again if you use an e-postcard. You can choose, write and send a card at any time of the day and all without leaving your comfort of your home. Electronic postcards, or e-postcards, are picture postcards that can be sent over the Internet from your computer in minutes. To receive an e-postcard, you must have an e-mail address. You can even send one to yourself. There are many web sites on the Internet that offer this as a free service. A good one can be found at http://www.apple.com/icards, which is part of the Apple Computer web site. Other e-postcard web sites include http://www.greetings.yahoo.com and http://www.egreetings.com.

Snail mail

Traditional mail sent across great distances is normally transported by plane. Even so, it can take a week for letters to reach Europe from North America. Traditional mail is nicknamed snail mail by Internet users, because it is so slow compared to e-mail.

POST AN E-CARD

You will need: *computer connected to the Internet, your friend's e-mail address.*

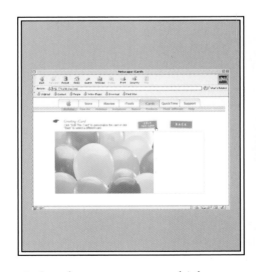

1 Open your Internet browser and connect to the Internet. Type in one of the addresses shown above to access the e-postcard web site. A page then shows you all the different cards.

2 Select a category by clicking on it. A new page opens, which will contain a selection of different cards in the category you chose. Click on the one you like.

3 Another page opens, which displays a larger version of the picture to let you see it better. If you are happy with it, click on the icon that says "Edit This Card."

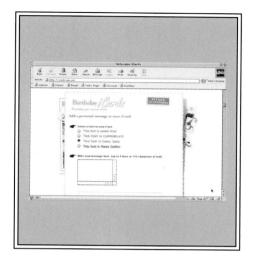

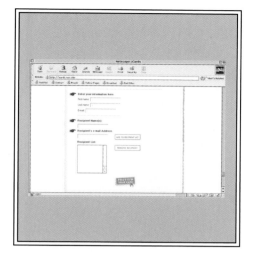

4 Choose a typeface that will suit your greeting card. When you have chosen a suitable typeface, type your message in the box at the bottom of the screen.

5 Fill in your name and e-mail address and your friend's name and e-mail address in the spaces provided so that the computer will know where to send the card.

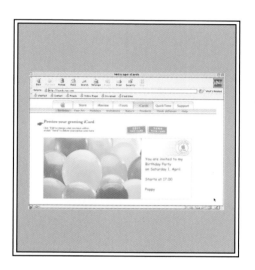

6 The computer then combines your message with the e-postcard and sends it to your friend. The computer will tell you if there has been a problem with the system and the card hasn't been delivered.

7 If you like, you can print any e-postcards that you receive and keep them just like birthday cards and Christmas cards. Collect as many different e-postcards as you can.

An e-journey

Whenever you send an e-mail, it travels down a telephone line to your ISP. Here, e-mails are sorted according to their destination and then sent by satellite to the recipient's ISP. It is then sent back down a telephone wire to the recipient of the e-mail. E-mails can arrive in minutes, but sometimes they are sent in batches and can take a few hours to reach their destination.

THE WORLD WIDE WEB

THE World Wide Web (www) has created huge interest in the Internet, because it makes it possible to access information from all over the world. The Internet and the www are not the same thing. The www is just a way of finding information on the Internet. The www is made up of millions of web sites about almost anything you can think of. Many organizations, colleges and schools have web sites, and there are a million others made by people just like you. You need an Internet browser to display web pages for you.

Web sites are much like a magazine. There is always a first page, similar to a magazine cover, which is called the home page. This displays a list of the web site's contents and allows you to explore your way around the web site.

Worldwide success

In 1990, an Englishman named Tim Berners-Lee developed the World Wide Web at the European Laboratory for Particle Physics in Switzerland (also known as CERN). He wrote the original HTML (Hypertext Mark-up Language) code. This enables web pages to be viewed on a computer. Today, the www is the most popular way of accessing information on the Internet, and it is used by millions of people throughout the world.

Web site addresses

Web addresses always start with http:// (hypertext transfer protocol), which is the way your computer reads web pages. Then comes www, followed by the domain name, which tells you where the web site can be found.

http://www.apple.com

YAHOOLIGANS!®

the Web Guide for Kids

Arts & Entertainment

Around the World

Computers & Games

Web sites

When you open a web site, the first page you will see is the home page. A home page such as Yahooligans! has a list of the site's contents, which will to help you to navigate your way around the web site. Yahooligans! is a site that acts as an Internet guide for young people. You can find all kinds of subjects, varying from information on arts and entertainment to computers and games. With a home computer and Internet access it is possible to answer such questions as "What is the capital of Peru?" or "Who was the first person in space?" in just a few minutes. There are web sites devoted to information on any subject you can think of, as well as commercial sites, which seem destined to change forever the way we do business.

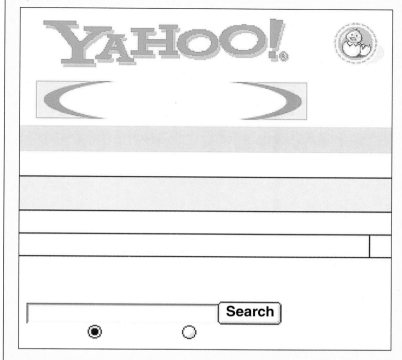

Search engines

Many people find that the Internet is one of the best ways to find out information. Unfortunately, searching the Internet for specific information can be difficult, because there are so many web sites that you might have to search through. In this situation, a search engine may be a handy tool. Yahoo! is just one of many search engines on the Internet. Simply type in your question in the text box on screen, and let Yahoo! do the work for you. Yahoo! also presents information in organized categories, such as science and sports, to make searching for information even easier. Just click on the category link and pick one of the sites. Despite their name, search engines are not really engines at all. They are a piece of automated software that search web sites, making a note of the essential information such as the site title, address and often the first line of text on the web site. This information is stored on a huge database, which can be accessed by the Internet user.

Servers

All the web pages on the www are stored on large, powerful computers known as servers. The picture to the right shows the main server room for the www in Geneva, Switzerland. Servers belong to the many different Internet Service Providers (ISPs). When a user types in the unique address of a web site using an Internet browser, the browser links to the server where the web site is stored and sends a GET command. It then tells the server to send all of the information needed to reconstruct the web pages on your own computer.

Web games

There are many Net game web sites, and some allow you to download games on to your computer and play with people from all around the world. Some games need special software called a plug-in, which may make the graphics of the game look much more realistic. You can download plug-ins free from games web sites.

WEB CULTURE

MUSEUMS house some of the world's finest collections of antiquities and art, but their one disadvantage is that they are spread out all over the world, so it is difficult to get to all of them. Thanks to the World Wide Web, however, you can see museums such as the Metropolitan Museum of Art in New York on your computer screen. Most museums have their own web sites, which include pictures of the galleries and the exhibits they contain. Some web sites allow you to take a "virtual tour" of the galleries, and you can zoom in to take a closer look at the exhibits. One of the most popular web sites of this type is that of the Louvre Museum in Paris, France (http://www.louvre.fr).

See Paris

When you visit the Louvre's web site, this is the image that you see. It is just as if you are visiting for real. In the 1990s, large parts of the Louvre were reconstructed to make the museum more accessible to visitors. The ground level entrance to the museum was relocated to the central courtyard, called the Cour Napoléon, and was crowned by a steel-and-glass pyramid designed by American architect I. M. Pei.

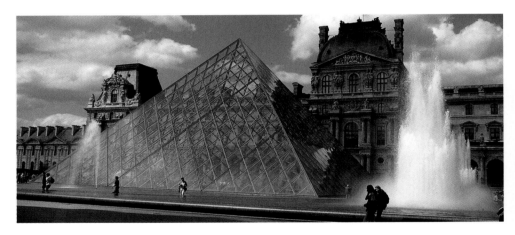

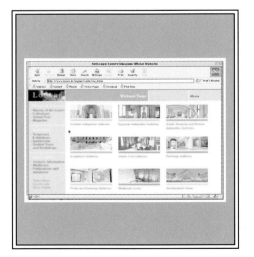

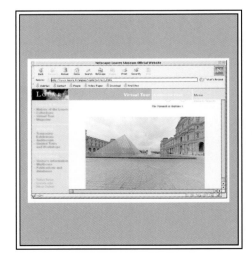

1 Open your Internet browser and connect to the Internet. Type in the web site address of the Louvre (http://www.louvre.fr). Click on the words "Discover Our Virtual Tour."

2 A new page offers you choices of different areas of the museum that you might want to visit. Choose "Architectural Views" to see the huge glass pyramid.

3 You need to download Quick-Time to view the pictures. Type http://www.quicktime.com. Follow the instructions. Then click on the icon next to "Pyramid at daytime 1."

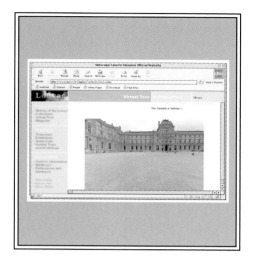

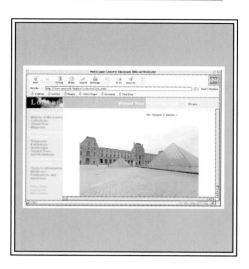

4 When the picture appears, look at the buildings by holding the mouse button down and dragging it over the picture. The picture moves to show you different views.

5 You can see the courtyard and the pyramid from different sides, as if you were walking round it. If you can't go to Paris to see it for yourself, this is the next best thing.

6 Return to the main menu and click on "Paintings Galleries." See the *Mona Lisa* by Leonardo da Vinci in the *Salle des Etats*. Move around and zoom in and out using the mouse.

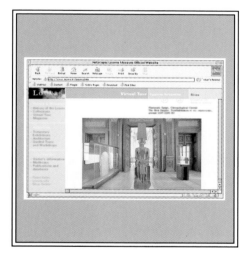

7 The Egyptian Antiquities Galleries are also good to look at. Again, use your mouse to move around the gallery and look at the exhibits up close.

8 You can also browse in a "virtual shop," which sells cards, posters, and books about some of the things you have seen in the museum.

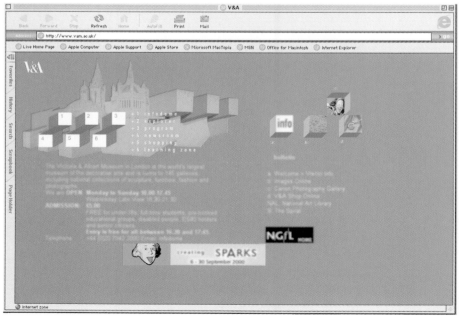

London museums online

The Victoria and Albert Museum in London in the United Kingdom is the world's largest museum of decorative arts, containing over 140 galleries of photography, sculpture, fashion, furniture, and painting. Many of the works of art can be viewed online, through the museum's web site. Access the web site by typing in www.vam.ac.uk. This takes you to the museum's home page. You can then choose to explore one of the galleries by pressing your mouse on the "Explorer" box. Not only will you be able to look at the works of art on the web site, but you can also find more information about them. Other web pages contain pictures of the museum's galleries, and you can also access the museum shop and buy reproductions of some of the pieces of art.

COMPUTERS IN EVERYDAY LIFE

COMPUTERS are used in all areas of our lives. They are found in shops, libraries, offices and in our homes. Most simple electronic machines, such as washing machines, microwave ovens and telephones, contain some kind of computer technology. Even a digital watch contains microchips. Some people worry that we are becoming too dependent on computer technology. Most, though, admit that computers make many things a lot easier and faster. It is amazing to think that computers were almost unheard of only 50 years ago. Today, almost everyone's lives are affected by computers in some form or another.

Bar codes

Many libraries use bar-code scanners that electronically scan bar codes printed on all their books. Bar codes consist of a number of parallel lines and spaces, which the reader scans and feeds back to the library's main computer. The bar code represents lots of data about the book, for example, its author, publisher and when it was published. This computer keeps a record of all this data. The computer also records who has borrowed the book and when they borrowed it, so the library staff will know when the books are due to be returned.

Computer-aided clothing

A clothing production designer uses computer-aided design (CAD) software to transfer the paper patterns seen at the lower left of the picture on to the computer screen. The shapes, or "nest," of patterns together form a single garment. CAD helps the production designer to check the different sizes and shapes of clothing before they are manufactured. CAD is used in many areas of industry. Systems generally consist of a computer with one or more work stations, featuring video monitors and interactive graphics-input devices.

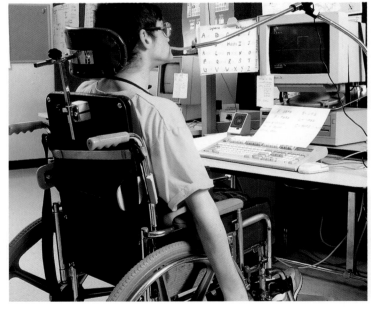

Computers and disabled people

This man is unable to use his arms, but he can still operate a computer by using a mouthpiece. Computers have made the lives of disabled people much easier than before. For example, the houses of people who have difficulty moving around can be set up so that many tasks, such as turning on a light switch, can be done using their computer.

Tracking flights

The air traffic control tower at Los Angeles Airport uses an array of computerized equipment to keep track of the positions of hundreds of aircraft. Air traffic is increasing every day. The technology used by air traffic controllers and pilots to avoid collisions and bad weather has had to become more sophisticated.

Medicine

A doctor uses a digital camera to photograph a man's eye for keeping with his medical records. The resulting image is displayed on the computer screen and is kept for analysis by other doctors. Medical specialists who may live far away can be consulted. This enables instant response and saves on travel costs.

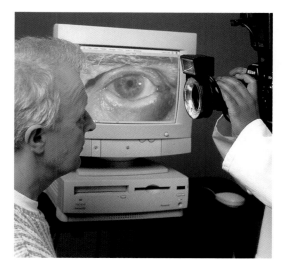

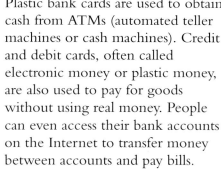

Computer banking

Plastic bank cards are used to obtain cash from ATMs (automated teller machines or cash machines). Credit and debit cards, often called electronic money or plastic money, are also used to pay for goods without using real money. People can even access their bank accounts on the Internet to transfer money between accounts and pay bills.

Growth of the Internet

Today, over 50 million people around the world own a personal computer. Soon, using the Internet will become as common as using the telephone. Even those people who do not have their own computer, or who are traveling, can find one to use. Many libraries have computers that can be used for free. Internet cafes, where you pay to connect to the Internet, are opening up all over the world. Today, you do not even have to own a computer to use the World Wide Web. Televisions and telephones have already been developed that connect to the Internet.

HEALTH AND ORGANIZATION

IT is essential to organize the space around your computer so you can use it properly. Keep all your papers in files and make sure your desk is tidy so you can use your keyboard easily and see the screen clearly to prevent muscle and eye strain. The project on the opposite page shows you how to make some files to help keep your work tidy.

Store your floppy disks and CDs in their covers when you are not using them to keep them clean and safe from scratches. The disks can also be affected by magnets, so do not put them on objects such as speakers, which have magnets in them. Positioning your computer is also important. If there is too much light shining on the screen, the glare will make it hard to see what you are doing.

Sitting position
You must sit comfortably when using a computer. Adjust the height of your seat to look down at the screen, and keep your back straight. Always take regular breaks if you are using the computer for a long time.

Eye strain

Staring at a computer screen for long periods of time is not good for you, because it will cause you to strain your eyes. Here are some eye exercises you can do to help prevent eye strain.

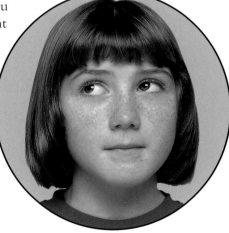

1 Keeping your head still, first move your eyes so that they are looking at the top right corner of the room.

2 Relax them for a moment. Then move your eyes to look at the top left corner of the room.

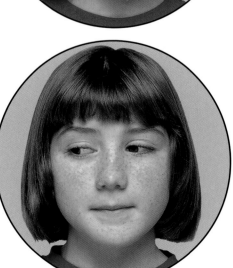

3 Relax again. Now move your eyes to look at the bottom right corner of the room.

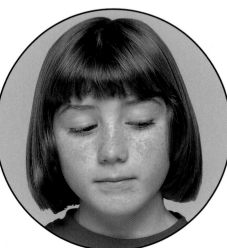

4 Relax once more. Finally, move your eyes to look at the bottom left corner of the room.

MAKING YOUR OWN FOLDERS

You will need:
one large piece and some small pieces of colored paper, black marker.

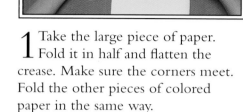

1 Take the large piece of paper. Fold it in half and flatten the crease. Make sure the corners meet. Fold the other pieces of colored paper in the same way.

2 You will end up with one large folder and four smaller ones. Draw a symbol on each folder to show what will be kept in it. You could either copy the ones above, or design your own.

3 For instance, you could draw an envelope on your letters folder, a paint palette for your paintings and drawings, a CD for your music homework, or a book for your essays.

4 Collect your papers together and sort them out into categories. Put each category into a different folder, so that you can find them easily.

5 Now put each small folder in the large one. This system of keeping things in folders is the one used by most computers. The large folder represents your computer's hard disk. The smaller folders represent the individual folders for different subjects.

6 To make a new folder on your computer, go to File in the menu bar and select New Folder if you are using a Mac or Folder if you are using a PC. A new folder will be created with the name bar highlighted ready for you to type in its name. Your work will be organized, so that you can find it easily.

CHANGING LIFESTYLES

COMPUTERS are becoming smaller, faster and more powerful all the time. Microprocessors have developed very rapidly in the last ten years, and it looks as if they will continue to do so. Data storage is improving all the time. In a few years, huge amounts of data will be stored on tiny pocket-size computers. Computers will become so small that they will be incorporated into the clothes that we wear. In fact, they have changed human life so much in recent years that it is difficult to imagine how they will be used in the future.

Growth of the Internet
Televisions and telephones that connect to the Internet are already in production. This is a WAP (wireless application protocol) phone, which means the user can access the Internet without connecting to a normal telephone line.

Computer glasses
This man is wearing an i-glass. It is a head-mounted display unit that links up to a tiny personal computer. Information is displayed as three-dimensional images on a color monitor in front of the man's eyes. Sound is heard through earphones. Data is inputted into the computer using a hand-held keyboard, a microphone or cameras attached to the man's clothing. This is truly mobile computing.

Computerized clothing
These futuristic outfits were designed by a team of fashion designers and computer scientists. The red outfit has a solar panel in the hat, which powers a mobile telephone. The chest brooch contains a device to stop the woman from getting lost, while the kneepads light up so that she can see where she is walking in the dark. The silver outfit can receive e-mail, which is played through earphones or projected on to the glasses.

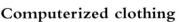

Wrist camera

The world's first mini digital wrist camera, the Casio WQV-1, was launched in January 2000. The camera can store up to 100 images, which can be viewed on the watch's screen. The images can then be stored, deleted or downloaded on to a PC for editing and archiving using the latest infrared technology.

FOODSTORE.COM

SEARCH

bananas

DEPARTMENTS

bread and cakes

breakfast cereals

canned goods

dairy

delicatessen

<u>fruits & vegetables</u>

jams and preserves

pasta and grains

ADD TO BASKET?

apples, cooking

bananas

grapes, seedless

oranges

pineapple

Internet shopping

Foodstore.com, shown above, is a fictional web site, but from the picture you can imagine just how easy it is to shop online. Just type in what you want to buy, and add it to your shopping basket. When paying for products on the Internet, you type your credit card details in to a secure form. This is checked by the Internet retailer, who will then arrange for the goods to be delivered to your door.

New working lifestyles

Once it was thought that people who worked together had to be in the same place. Today, the Internet allows people from all over the world to work together. By using video conferencing, they can see each other on their computer monitors, and they can also have a live conversation.

Movies on a disk

Sony's new Digital Versatile Disc (DVD) player allows you to watch the latest feature films on a disk the size of a conventional CD. DVDs may contain a combination of video, audio, and computer data, but the advantage lies in the fact that they can hold up to seven times as much data as a typical CD.

GLOSSARY

application
Computer software that is designed for a specific type of activity, such as word-processing, desktop publishing, or manipulating graphics.

binary code
The digital code that computers use, which is made up of just two numbers, "0" and "1." Combinations of "0" and "1" can be used to represent any kind of information, such as text or images.

bit
The smallest amount of computer information such as a 0 or 1 in binary code.

bitmap
An image that is built out of tiny dots of different color and tone. They can be edited dot by dot.

browser
A piece of software that finds and displays web pages and other documents stored on the Internet. Examples of browser software are Netscape Navigator and Internet Explorer.

byte
One letter or number in binary code. A byte is 8 bits.

CD-ROM (compact disc read-only memory)
A disk similar to an audio CD that stores information data that can only be read.

Colossus
The first fully electronic computer built during World War II by Englishman Alan Turing. Its purpose was to decode enemy messages.

CPU (central processing unit)
The "brain" of the computer, which contains the processing chips and electronic circuits.

cursor
The arrow on a monitor that indicates where on the screen you are working. Can also be used to select options from windows on screen.

data
Pieces of information.

database
An organized store of information.

desktop
The main interface of the operating system that is shown on the screen after the computer has started up and before any programs are running. Use it to access everything on the computer.

desktop publishing (DTP)
Creating magazines, newspapers, or any other printed material using a desktop computer and page-layout software.

digital
Any device that utilizes binary code is described as being digital. All computers are digital.

disk drive
The device that holds, reads, and writes on to a disk such as a floppy or Zip disk.

document
An electronic file that contains text, pictures, or any other kind of data that can be inputted into a computer.

downloading
Copying files, such as web pages or software, from the Internet to your computer's hard disk.

e-mail (electronic mail)
A way of sending messages from one computer to another using the Internet.

ENIAC
One of the first electronically operated computers, which was built by American engineers John Atansoff, Presper Eckert, and John Mauchly in 1943.

file
A document in digital form that is stored either on the computer's hard disk or on an external disk. It can contain words and pictures.

filter
A special effect that can be applied to a graphics image, such as a texture or a distortion. Usually found in paint or photo-manipulation applications, such as Adobe Photoshop.

floppy disk
A portable data-storage disk. Floppies hold about 1.4MB of data and so are only really useful for storing text files.

folder
A storage place for computer files. Folders can store anything from applications to your personal work. Folders can be created and thrown away at any time.

gigabyte
One billion (a thousand million) bytes or characters.

hard disk
A computer's main storage disk, which holds the operating system and application files.

hardware
The equipment that makes up a computer—disk drives, processor, monitor, keyboard, mouse, printer, etc.

home page
An introductory page that contains links to other pages on a web site.

HTML (hypertext mark-up language)
The computer code that makes text and graphics appear on a web site in an interactive way.

HTTP (hypertext transfer protocol)
The language computers use to transfer web pages over the Internet. When followed by a colon (:) and two forward slashes (//) it forms the first part of a full web address or uniform resource locator (URL).

icon
A tiny picture on which you click to make your computer do a task. Icons also tell you that your computer is busy.

insertion point
A flashing line that appears on the screen when words are being written to show where they will begin.

Internet
A worldwide computer network that is made up of many smaller networks of computers that can all communicate with each other.

ISP (Internet Service Provider)
One of the companies through which Internet connection is made.

kilobyte
One thousand characters or bytes.

laptop
A portable computer that is powered by a rechargeable battery.

layout
The arrangement of text and pictures on a page.

megabyte
One million characters or bytes.

menu
A list of options from which a user can select something.

microprocessor
A single chip containing all the elements of a computer's CPU.

modem (modulator/demodulator)
A device that allows computer data to be sent down a telephone line.

monitor
A screen used to display the computer's visual output.

mouse
A computer input device that translates its movements into the movement of the cursor on the screen. So called because it is roughly mouse-size and has a "tail" wire that links it to the computer.

multimedia
A combination of text, graphics, sound, animation, and video.

OS (operating system)
The main piece of software needed by all computers to allow them to function properly.

pixel
A dot of light out of which the images on a computer screen are made.

RAM (random access memory)
Computer memory that holds data temporarily until the computer is switched off.

resolution
The number of shades of color that a computer monitor can display. The higher the number, the more the eye is tricked into seeing a clearer and smoother image.

ROM (read-only memory)
A type of computer memory that holds information permanently.

scanner
A device used to scan and record data

silicon chip
A small piece of the chemical element silicon on which are etched thousands of tiny electrical circuits.

software
Applications that enable computers to carry out specific tasks.

URL (uniform resource locator)
The address of a web site on the Internet.

virtual reality (VR)
The process by which computers are used to create an artificial place that looks real.

web page
A computer document written in HTML, which is linked to other web pages.

web site
A collection of web pages.

WWW (World Wide Web)
A huge collection of information that is available on the Internet. The information is divided up into web pages that are linked together.

Zip disk
A portable data storage disk that comes in two storage sizes—100MB and 250MB.

INDEX